THE PASSION OF COMMAND
THE MORAL IMPERATIVE OF LEADERSHIP

COLONEL B.P. MCCOY

Introduction by Bing West,
author of *No True Glory: A Frontline Account of the Battle for Fallujah*

Front cover photo: by Bryan Mangan
Back cover photo: by Kuni Takahashi/Boston Herald/ReflexNews
Into Baghdad, 7 April, 2003. Marines of Task Force 3rd Battalion 4th Marines
rush across the makeshift repairs of the Diyala Bridge and enter Baghdad.

Special thanks to the staff of the Marine Corps Association for the
publishing of *The Passion of Command*. Of note, was the leadership of Col James
Walt Davis, USMC (Ret); administrative assistant, Laura Casey; editor and proof-
reader, MaryAnn Preston; typesetter, Patty Everett; production manager, Jon Dodd
and designer, Steve Parrish.

Published by the
Marine Corps Association
Box 1775
Quantico, Virginia 22134
(703) 640-6161

First Edition
April 2007

ISBN 0-940328-37-2

Printed in the United States of America
by the Marine Corps Association

To order copies of this book:
www.mca-marines.org
1-888-237-7683

WARNING:
WITHOUT GENUINE CONCERN
THIS IS ALL WORTHLESS

---

*BODY AND SPIRIT I SURRENDERED WHOLE TO
HARSH INSTRUCTORS—AND RECEIVED A SOUL.*
—RUDYARD KIPLING

Many thanks go out to a long list of friends, mentors and leaders with whom I have been blessed to serve. Either directly by assisting in the preparation of this monograph, or indirectly through years of mentoring and guidance, they have contributed to my education and development as an officer of Marines. Colonel Walt Davis, Lieutenant Colonel Phil Skuta, Lieutenant Colonel Harry Tunnell USA, Colonel Royal Mortenson, Doctor Lani Kass, Ph.D., Colonel Jim Harris, Lieutenant Colonel "Big John" Morrow, Lieutenant General Jack Klimp, General Peter Pace, Gunnery Sergeant Bob Newman, Gunnery Sergeant Jack Coughlin, Major Matt Baker, Major Andy Petrucci, Colonel David Close, Colonel John Keenan, Brigadier General Keith Holcomb, Brigadier General John Kelly, Brigadier General John Allen, Sergeant J.A. Carroll, Major General Ray Smith, Mr. Bing West, Master Gunnery Sergeant Barry Walker, Gunner Terry Walker, Gunner Gene Coughlin, Colonel Kip Haskell, Colonel Craig Tucker, Lieutenant General James N. Mattis, Brigadier General Steve Hummer, Brigadier General Joe Dunford, Major General Tom Jones, Gunnery Sergeant Jean-Paul Courville, and Lieutenant Colonel Steve Corcoran. Much thanks and admiration to a special friend and mentor Lieutenant Colonel Al Christy. Without his advice and diligent and painstaking efforts in editing, this work would never have been completed.

The success of the battalion is owed entirely to the men of the battalion and specifically to the non-commissioned officers, staff non-commissioned officers, and junior officers who carried the burden of leadership through the long, hot days and nights of training in 29 Palms, California, and into the crucible of combat. By their strength and courage, and that of our sister battalions, we succeeded.

A special debt of gratitude also is owed to Sergeant Major Dave Howell, the heart and soul of 3rd Battalion, 4th Marines, who taught me what real small-unit leadership was all about.

**Author proceeds from this book will be donated to the
Injured Marine Semper Fi Fund.
www.SemperFiFund.org**

SAEPIUS EXERTUS, SEMPER FIDELIS,

FRATER INFINITAS.

OFTEN TESTED, ALWAYS FAITHFUL,

BROTHERS FOREVER.

Dedicated to the courageous Marines and Sailors of 3rd Battalion, 4th Marines: You always gave your very best. No matter how much I tried to give, you gave double. When I redoubled my efforts, you responded tenfold. I am forever and hopelessly in your debt. Just being among you, and being called your commander, made me a better man and Marine. For that reason, I must acknowledge that I will never again be as good as a man or Marine as I was those two years we were together. To our brothers who gave the last full measure, may they never be forgotten. For the rest, you courageous souls of the battalion, may you look upon your scars—seen and unseen—and remember the great deeds of your youth.

In Memoriam

Lance Corporal William W. White	29 March 2003	Ad Diwaniya
Corporal Mark A. Evnin	3 April 2003	Al Kut
Lance Corporal Andrew J. Aviles	7 April 2003	Diyala
Corporal Martin A. Medellin	7 April 2003	Diyala
Corporal Jesus A. Gonzalez	12 April 2003	Baghdad
Corporal Jason D. Mileo	14 April 2003	Baghdad
Corporal Daniel R. Amaya	11 April 2004	Fallujah
Lance Corporal Torrey L. Grey	11 April 2004	Fallujah
First Lieutenant Oscar Jimenez	11 April 2004	Fallujah
Corporal Bob W. Roberts	17 May 2004	Haditha

In 2003, the 1st Marine Division attacked from Kuwait to Baghdad, shifting east to seize Iraq's southern oilfields, then northwest in a drive straight toward Baghdad, then cutting northeast in a end run around Baghdad's outer defenses. From Baghdad, a task force drove north to Takrit. Taking into account these feints and excursions, the Blue Diamond raced more than 1200 kilometers in 20 days, among the longest sustained blitzkriegs in history. The sole pause of 36 hours was ordered by CentCom, under protest by the Marine Expeditionary Force. In 2004, the division returned to Iraq and undertook counterinsurgency operations in the fractious Sunni province of Al Anbar, west of Baghdad.

These two different types of operations – an armored offensive that bypassed as many enemy units as possible and an infantry occupation of hostile towns and cities – occurred so close in time that the same set of Marines participated in both. This book is an accurate distillation of the keys to unit success under markedly different circumstances. Colonel McCoy put in the time and mental sweat to organize this primer on how to prepare any combat arms unit for battle in the early 21st Century. On a larger plane, though, McCoy would be the first to say he didn't write it; the division did. The principles in here are echoed by dozens of others; Mattis, Kelly, Hummer, Dunford, Toolan, Dowdy, Tucker, Conlin, Malay, L'Etoile, O'Donahue, Lopez, Howell, Mayer, Buhl, Brandl, Coughlin, Cargile, and Ramos.

What makes this small book exceptional is its heritage. It is the new generation of front line combat leaders speaking in direct, no-nonsense sentences to the company and platoon commanders, to the gunnery sergeants, platoon sergeants and squad leaders. When it is time to prepare for war at the battalion level, this is how to do it.

The reader will quickly get the gist. This is about how to instill spirit and the habits of discipline. Colonel Tucker and others refer to this as "being brilliant in the basics". The essentials of this book focus on coordinated action during combat when bullets are cracking by. That is an unusual unifying theme, singularly apt and often overlooked.

Not to trivialize the subject matter, but an analogy might be reading a book about professional football written by a quarterback who starts with the ball having been snapped. As he backpedals and reads the field, he calls a timeout, the moment freezes and he explains to you, the reader, everything that is going through his head, where he expects his blockers and receivers to be, how the defense is reacting, what plays he has in mind, how he evaluates risk – reward for going long versus short, why he knows where his receivers are going to be three seconds from now and what factors count most in his decision.

In other words, he's working backwards from his desired end state – an eventual touchdown – to explain how a team must train and think to get there. Once in the midst of the game, a dozen critical sub-plays are being made simultaneously. The quarterback knows all this and can rely on ten other players (units) to respond in a predictable way with no further signals or coaching. On the field, it's all about executing and adapting via brevity codes (signals and plays).

Given thorough training and practice, what really happens in combat depends on spirit and intensity. Each player knows what he has to do. It is time to execute. This book emphasizes that mental spirit – that mental zone that is combat, engaging an enemy intent on killing you. No one thinks of the basics at that moment; instead, you execute them by rote. You are either directing fire or maneuvering while others support you by fire. In either case, you instinctively rely on your teammates to have it all together. *Trained instinct.*

Hesitation on a battlefield stems from two causes. The first is enemy fire superiority. You are outmatched or out of position and moving forward will result in more casualties while not increasing the odds of taking the objective. In most instances today (as distinct from, say, WWII), American firepower and communications render this condition unlikely to in most firefights. When it does happen, commonsense suggests seeking cover and getting on the radio.

The second reason for hesitation is uncertainty inside one unit (squad, platoon) about what it or an adjacent unit is expected to do as the bullets snap by. Colonel McCoy does a superb job of stopping the action, explaining it like a quarterback and instilling in the reader an understanding that freezing up will not happen if the right set of basics have been instilled and repeated over and over.

It takes about two months for the mind and the body to develop a true habit, whether it be daily running in preparation for a marathon or writing a thousand words a day to produce a book. To develop the teamwork and automatically react in the ultimate contest – battle – a unit needs to train together for three to four months assuming qualifications in all the requisite combat arms skills already exist.

I had the privilege of observing McCoy's battalion – as well as those of Malay, Mayer O''Donahue, Brandl, L'Etoile, Lopez and others – in various firefights. Singularly striking were the quick adjustments, the short, verbal bursts over the radios followed by immediate actions to apply fire or shift units. The battalions were teams with different mounted and dismounted units acting independently and yet in unison – result being a fluidity that only months of training and faith in a system could insure.

Indeed, the highest compliment to the principles McCoy espouses occurred after his battalion had left Iraq. McCoy writes about the march up to Baghdad in April of 2003 and the first battle of Fallujah in April of 2004. At the second battle of Fallujah in November, the battalions led by Buhl, Malay, Brandl and Ramos attacked abreast across six kilometers against 1500 jihadists, advancing south for ten days, calling in over 5,000 rounds of artillery and 500 air strikes – with not one fatality from friendly fire. That required extraordinary teamwork.

While McCoy does not specify a particular type of battlefield, it is clear he was referring to offensive operations by friendly troops supported by vehicles in open and urban terrain versus dismounted troops. If the setting were the jungles of Vietnam or the shores of Iwo Jima, the book would be less apt. The framework presented herein applies to Iraq and more generally, to flat, populated terrain. A bit more generically, it applies to conditions where the Marine commander has a view of the battlefield and excellent electronic – voice and digital maps – communications with his subordinates.

The military historians John Keegan and Victor Hanson have stressed what gives the West its edge in battle since Gaugamela in Iraq in 323 BC is culture, not technology. For instance, the Mongols introduced the mounted blitzkrieg and China invented gunpowder. Yet the West has prevailed in the wars that have defined the growth of civilization and set the boundaries of nations, religions and empires. Hanson specifically attributes this edge in decisive battles to the Western culture of peer leadership – those who share in the risks share in the decision-making, including critiquing the decisions of their superiors. This atmosphere fosters adaptability and unit confidence in its leaders and in each other.

This book is the practical, tactical primer that validates Keegan and Hanson. Time and again, McCoy returns to one unifying organizational principle: there is no i in team. Instead, there is a shared bond of responsibility for insuring individual competence and unit integrity and cohesion. Everyone knows the plays and has a voice in assessing them.

Like any large organization, the Marine Corps has some who "fail upward" and emerge autocratic and uncorrected in a position of authority on a battlefield. But there are few of them. The Marine Corps is the most disciplined – and to outsiders, rigid – in its rank structure. Discipline is based on the insistence that there is a right versus wrong way of behaving. Discipline is what gives the junior NCO the confidence to insist that a firefight be conducted the right way. Instinctively, we understand that in a tight situation, the senior Marine can point to all other Marines, yell an order and all will obey, no matter what their particular unit. Why? Because all Marines share a faith in their battlefield system.

This book stresses the organizational compact – the rifleman will do his part and the leader will include the voices of all in preparation for battle. This battle becomes the ultimate test of the unit's cohesion. The principles put forth are sound. The freshness of the book lies in its post-battle candor. It isn't one person writing; it is the collective voice of several battalions. It is most interesting because it is written from the viewpoint of a leader standing in the middle of a firefight, then flashing back to the training and planning that insured the outcome of the battle.

—Bing West, Author of *No True Glory: A Frontline Account of the Battle for Fallujah*

CONTACT!

IF I HAD THE TIME AND ANYTHING LIKE YOUR ABILITY TO STUDY WAR, I THINK I SHOULD CONCENTRATE ALMOST ENTIRELY ON THE ACTUALITIES OF WAR—THE EFFECTS OF TIREDNESS, HUNGER, FEAR, LACK OF SLEEP, WEATHER. ... THE PRINCIPLES OF STRATEGY AND TACTICS, AND THE LOGISTICS OF WAR ARE ABSURDLY SIMPLE: IT IS THE ACTUALITIES THAT MAKE WAR SO COMPLICATED AND SO DIFFICULT, AND ARE USUALLY SO NEGLECTED BY HISTORIANS.

—LORD WAVELL TO LIDDELL HART

With all the menace of a giant shark in search of prey, our armored column steadily churns eastward on Iraq's Highway 6, paralleling the Tigris River toward the town of Al Kut. Along the ancient banks of the Tigris, we follow in the footsteps of the Akkadians, Sumerians, Hittites, Kassites, Assyrians and Persians. We trace the path of Alexander the Great and his army of Macedon. They were succeeded by the Parthians, Sassanians, the Arabs and then the Mongols led by Hulagu Khan. After the Mongols came the Ottoman Turks and finally the British Army. Today, it is the Americans. It is midmorning, 3 April 2003. Task Force, 3rd Battalion, 4th Marines is on the attack for the 14th day in a row.

Our mission is to destroy the remaining offensive capabilities of the Republican Guard's Baghdad Infantry Division. In short, we are to remove the enemy from the game board, allowing the rest of the 1st Marine Division to turn its back to Al Kut and continue the march to Baghdad. Our task force is comprised of roughly 1,150 Sailors and Marines and 165 vehicles, 75 armored, to include 15 formidable M1-A1 tanks, or "Tigers," as we call them. Bravo Company is our tank unit and has been complemented with an attached infantry platoon from Kilo Company, under the command of Second Lieutenant Kaloha Stokes. With the Tigers' inherent protection and fire power, they typically have led the task force in these "movement to contact" operations, since the thick skin of the tanks can take a hit better than anything else we own. "Movement to contact" is military parlance for "go find the enemy and develop the situation." In doing so, it is not uncommon for the enemy, hiding in a stationary position on ground of his choosing, to get off the first shot. In this particular scenario we know that after we make contact with the Baghdad Infantry Division, the enemy will suffer the complete destruction of its remaining armor and artillery, which will render any remaining infantry powerless to affect the 1st Marine Division's drive on Baghdad. What we do not know right now is the location, composition, and/or disposition of the enemy. We will accomplish this the old-fashioned way: "Find 'em, fix 'em & fight 'em."

We have been on the move nearly constantly for 16 days—since 19 March, a full two days prior to the 21 March assault into Iraq. Our task force has fought thus far at Al Basra, Hajil, Afak, Al Budair, and Ad Diwaniya and endured an epic sandstorm on the 24th and 25th of March. We are now exhausted from the effort of constant movement, punctuated by moments of fighting and killing along the way. For the first three days of the offensive, nobody had slept. Since then, no man has benefited from more than three or four hours of sleep in each 24-hour period—usually taken in multiple catnaps. Personally, I slept perhaps an hour and a half the previous night and maybe a total of eight hours or so over the past three days. Each day of fighting has been the equivalent of completing a major physical endurance event such as a marathon, with the added bonus of the nervous system's parasympathetic response to extreme exertion, stress, and doses of adrenaline, where the body and mind crash afterward in an effort to recoup from the effort. Adding to the tally of stress is the uncertainty of the day-to-day situation and the ever-increasing threat of the enemy's use of chemical weapons as we close in on Baghdad. Today we will cross north of the Tigris River and the "red line" where intelligence has estimated that Saddam would be compelled to use chemical weapons to defend his capital city. For more than two weeks, we have been living and sleeping in our hot, bulky, charcoal-lined chemical protective suits that resist every movement. Even urination requires extra effort. Every man is filthy in spite of our valiant efforts at hygiene. We do remain clean-shaven and keep our weapons maintained in spotless condition. The previous night has been spent digging the task force into defensive positions, reporting and coordinating our efforts with our higher headquarters, Regimental Combat Team-7, repairing and refueling vehicles in the pitch-black darkness and being ever careful to avoid the enemy mines that we have found sharing the field with us. Around midnight, we receive our mission to destroy the Baghdad Infantry Division elements south of the Tigris. By 0200, the order has changed to north of the Tigris. "Semper Gumby," mutters a red-eyed staff officer, so exhausted his speech is slurred. His quip regarding always being flexible might have been comical, if not for the fact that the lives of our men are at stake. With fatigue-numbed minds, we rapidly work to amend our plan, racing against the 0600 time of attack.

Crossing the line of departure right on time, we cover nearly 40 kilometers by 0900. Encountering only light resistance, we are now on the outskirts of Al Kut. Contact is imminent, yet the lure of sleep is so enticing it is nearly impossible to resist. I think of how nice it would be to lay my head against the sharp, metal radio mount to my left and close my eyes for just a few minutes. My radio crackles.

"Darkside 6, this is Bravo 6. Phase Line Saw. Time now. 15 KPH. Negative contact. Out!" "Bravo 6" is the Commanding Officer of Bravo Company, Captain Brian Lewis, an exceptionally dedicated officer who is loved by his men. Lewis is calling me by my call sign to let me know his location, speed, and enemy situation. The report is really for the task force command post, since I am only 20 meters behind Lewis's tank in my HMMWV (high-mobility, multipurpose, wheeled vehicle). Lewis's tank is behind the lead tank platoon, known as "Red Platoon." I respond, "Roger, out."

It takes an extra second for my brain to register the enemy RPK machine-gun tracers flying over the hood of my HMMWV. I yell, "Contact right—troops!" to

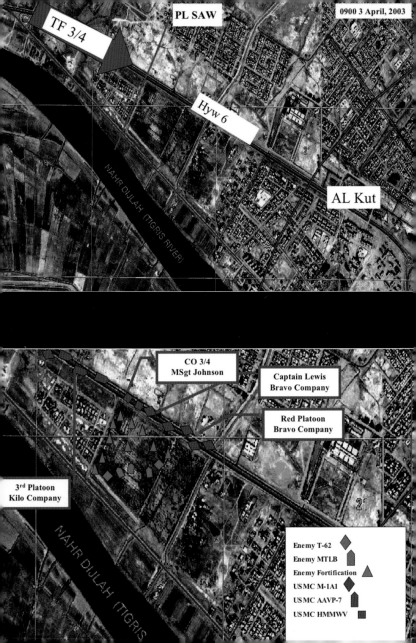

0900 3 April, 2003

TF 3/4

PL SAW

Hyw 6

NAHR DJLAH (TIGRIS RIVER)

AL Kut

CO 3/4
MSgt Johnson

Captain Lewis
Bravo Company

Red Platoon
Bravo Company

3rd Platoon
Kilo Company

NAHR DJLAH (TIGRIS)

Enemy T-62
Enemy MTLB
Enemy Fortification
US MC M-1A1
US MC AAVP-7
US MC HMMWV

Kill Zone

Ambush initiated/ Evnin killed	1
3rd Plt Kilo moves and dismounts	2
3rd Plt Kilo clears fortified positions/ AAVs support by fire	3
Kilo company moves to support	4
SSgt Popaditch overruns enemy	5
Red Plt kills enemy in canal	6
Red Plt destroys enemy counter attacks	7

Enemy T-62

Enemy MTLB

Enemy Fortification

USMC M-1A1

USMC AAVP-7

USMC HMMWV

Al Kut Fire Fight. Having gained fire superiority Marines advance behind machinegun, rocket and grenade fire. Note the smoke and dust from freshly detonated grenades.

Al Kut Fire Fight. Marine finishes two enemy fighters in their hole. Note the dust and smoke from the grenade that has just detonated and the brass ejecting from the M-16.

Al Kut Fire Fight. The two fighters killed in the previous photo.

Al Kut Fire Fight. 3rd Platoon Kilo Company consolidates in the palm grove. Note the

Al Kut Fire Fight. Marines of 3rd Platoon Kilo Company sweep past dead enemy fighters during consolidation of the palm grove.

Al Kut Fire Fight. 2nd Lt Kealoha Stokes radios his squads during the consolidation of the

Al Kut Fire Fight. Corporal Irish is given first aid for a gunshot wound to the shoulder before being evacuated. His life was saved by the ceramic plate in his flack vest that stopped two other rounds that would have penetrated his chest.

Al Kut Fire Fight. A Marine is evacuated from the battlefield on a CH-46 of HMM 364 "Purple Foxes". Note the teamwork and uniformity of the litter team.

Photo of Corporal Mark Evnin on Highway 1.

Father Devine, Regimental Chaplain, RCT-7, holds mass for members of 3/4 during a brief

The strain of battle. 2nd Lieutenant A.C. Lee Platoon Commander 1st Platoon India Company 3rd Battalion 4th Marine Regiment. Lee was one of the toughest and most fit Marines
in the battalion, note the strain and fatigue on his face during the April 6 battle at A Za'

9 April, 2003 Firdos Square Baghdad. An Iraqi citizen hands up the American Flag to Corporal Chin moments before the Saddam statue is brought down by the M-88 tank retriever of Bravo Company.

Easter Sunday 2003. 3/4 holds a memorial service for our dead. They were Black, White and Hispanic, Jews and Gentiles, tankers, trackers and grunts.

LtCol B.P. McCoy and Capt Kevin Norton in discussion on Highway 1.

One of the countless battle drill rehearsals conducted in the Mojave desert in 29 Palms California. A 60mm mortar squad of Kilo Company disembark to get their gun into action.

SgtMaj David C. Howell, the heart and soul of the Battalion, 9 April 2003, Baghdad.

One of the countless practice grenades thrown during training in the Mojave Desert. Marines engaged the enemy with "blue death" practice grenades from various positions, distances and differing target arrays simulating bunkers, trenches and fighting positions.

Lance Corporal Samuel Baynes, my M240G (7.62 mm medium machine gun) HMMWV turret gunner, directing his return fire into the date-palm grove on the right side of the road. "Right turn! Right turn and stop!" I tell the driver, Corporal Omar Monge. The idea is to put the engine block and ballistic glass of the HMMWV between the RPK and us. Instead, Monge turns left and stops. We are now positioned broadside to the enemy, with nothing but eighth-inch fiberglass for protection. It might as well have been an eighth-inch of butter. I give Monge a look he later describes as "the same look a dog gives its owner while the dog gets a bath—the "Why me? What did I ever do to you?" look. The second burst from the RPK hits low into the road embankment a few feet to my right, spraying dirt and chunks of asphalt into our faces. We bail out of the vehicle and immediately return as much fire as possible into the enemy positions. The enemy has let Red Platoon pass and initiates the ambush as soon as Lewis's tank, my HMMWV, and Master Sergeant Allan Johnson's HMMWV have entered the kill zone. The date-palm grove harbors a pair of dug-in T-62 tanks, three armored personnel carriers with machine guns, and expertly constructed and camouflaged bunkers. Also, there are trenches manned by more than 40 Iraqi combatants, which are a mix of Republican Guard and Saddam Fedayeen, also known as "Saddam's men of sacrifice," who often find their nerve to fight only under the influence of courage-building narcotics.

The enemy has initiated contact from as close as 30 meters, peppering the column with small-arms fire and rocket-propelled grenades. I can hear the radio and my own voice loud and clear, my brain all but squelching the deafening reports of weapons and the explosions of RPGs and tank main gun fire. In a semi-detached manner I recognize this as the phenomenon of auditory exclusion, or tunnel hearing, in which the brain, responding to stress and hormonally increased heart rate, filters out the unnecessary and processes the essential. I never cease to marvel at this adaptation of the mind, and it is comforting to recognize it for what it is. "Darkside, this is Darkside-6. Contact right. Phase line Saw. Out!" I am now reduced to being a rifleman. In the middle of the kill zone, I manage to get off one quick contact report to the Darkside Task Force. This contact report will initiate a sequence of actions based on habits formed by long months of training, endless rehearsals, and an implicit understanding of one another that has come from hours upon hours of discussions and exercises, some of which have been accomplished over a few beers at the bar.

Captain Russ Boyce, the peerless task force fire, support coordinator, currently located with the command post, will soon have artillery, close air support, and our own mortars weighing in on the fight. Captain Kevin Norton, the ever-aggressive Commanding Officer of Kilo Company, or Kilo 6, with an attached tank platoon, will be moving up to support Lewis's infantry platoon and closing the 200-meter gap to the kill zone.

It is called a "kill zone" for a reason. You do not want to be in one. The tactics, techniques, and procedures for counter-ambush drills when caught in a kill zone are very clear: Return as much fire as possible, and get out of the kill zone as soon as possible. The terrain here along the Tigris and Euphrates rivers features irrigated fields, criss-crossed with canals and raised levee roads. Such topography is terrible for mechanized vehicles and makes it nearly impossible for us to clear out of the kill zone. Those of us in it will now have to fight it out until the rest of Bravo arrives to even the odds. Lance Corporal Garfield Shealy, my radio operator, kneels next to me wearing the man-pack radio, steadily returning fire. The enemy has strong fortifications, with good fields of fire, and has anchored his left flank on the Tigris River and his right flank on a canal separating the palm grove from the city of Al Kut.

I grab the AN/PRC-119 radio handset from Shealy's backpack. Only seconds have passed, but I can already feel the effects of adrenaline coursing through my system. There is nothing worse than a shrill radio call. My heart is pounding. I take a deep breath in an attempt to bring my heart rate under control and look at my hands; they are steady enough to hold my rifle in one and the handset in the other. I squeeze the handset and give my directions to Kilo 6 and a brief update to the task force command post. I call for Kilo 6 to attack the seam between the Tigris River and the palm grove to get behind the enemy in order to unhinge his right flank. Thankfully, my voice seems steady and calm and belies the fact that my heart is beating like a drum in my chest. "That is a relief," I think to myself. Calm can be just as contagious as panic.

Bravo's Red Platoon is engaging the extreme eastern edge of the ambush, fighting off RPG teams and a platoon of enemy T-62 tanks, attempting to catch them in the flank from Al Kut. The enemy's plan is clear, and it is sound. He intends to pin us down in the kill zone and attack into our flanks with armor and RPG teams, a classic hammer and anvil. If we panic or hesitate, they will be successful.

Back in the kill zone, I clearly see the winking muzzle flashes of more than a dozen enemy weapons sweeping the road with fire. I return fire into the closest enemy, an RPK machine-gunner, probably the one who had initially opened up on my vehicle and who is now fully concentrating his fire not on just Lewis's tank, but on Lewis himself. Lewis is popping up and down in his hatch, directing the fire of his gunner as the RPK's rounds splatter and spark against his tank all around his cupola, giving a nearly comical impression of a game of "Whack-a-Mole." Lewis's tank hammers nine 120 mm main gun rounds into the palm grove in rapid succession: WHAM, WHAM, WHAM! I empty two magazines from my M-16A2 rifle into the enemy's muzzle flashes. We desperately try to match the enemy's fire power and reduce their accuracy to stay alive long enough until support arrives. I look left to Lewis's tank as the enemy RPK gives a long burst that throws a shower of sparks off Lewis's cupola hatch and the .50 caliber machine gun he mans. He disappears into the hatch. He does not pop back up. I fear the worst, but his tank remains in action, firing. Vegetation obscures my observation of the RPK's crew. I do not have a clear shot, but I can see the stream of tracers it produces. I fire into the vegetation at what I estimate to be its origin, hoping to suppress the crew—to make them duck and cover. Further to my left, Master Sergeant Johnson has the angle on the RPK and empties one magazine wildly at the enemy. Reloading, he scolds himself and recites the rifle-range mantra, "Front sight post, front sight post—squeeze." His next shots are well-aimed killing shots into the heads of the crew. That gun is now silent.

Bravo's infantry platoon comes roaring up in three armored amphibious vehicles (AAVs), slamming to a halt at the edge of the kill zone. Their heavy M2 .50 caliber machine guns and MK-19 40 mm automatic grenade launchers open up to cover the Marine infantry rushing down the back ramps of the 26-ton vehicles, as a volley of RPGs is unleashed by the enemy, some sailing high, while another ricochets off the hull and spins and hisses on the ground without detonating.

What happens next is pure violence, yet elegant in its harmony. Thirty-five U.S. Marines of Kilo Company's 3rd Platoon rush out of the gloomy confines of their AAVs and into the teeth of the enemy fire. They know nothing of the enemy's strength or disposition. All they know is that this is a "contact right" battle drill, and this is what we do in "contact right." Private First Class Dusty Ladendorf, one of the platoon's riflemen, is less than a year out of high school. In an after-action review he makes this comment on the firefight: "You come out of the back of the track and just do it like you were trained. Execute your battle drill, take cover and fire, cover your buddy's move, and move yourself when he covers you. Find the enemy, close in on him, and kill him. Keep moving and keep killing, until it's over." The platoon rushes straight into the teeth of the fire and gains a foothold in the palm grove, taking advantage of the protection provided by every subtle fold in the ground and clod of dirt.

An untrained observer may look at this scene and think it no more organized than a riot. Actually, to us it is ferocious poetry. Every weapon system joins the fight, each supporting the other: Machine guns, rifles, grenade launchers, and rocket launchers systematically suppress and then kill the enemy. We are now gaining fire superiority. Soon it is for the enemy to question the prospect of survival. It is a scene nearly as old as time itself. A pack of predators methodically corrals and slaughters its prey. It is brutal harmony, and no man here flinches from the task. I turn and see Corporal Mark Evnin, ten feet away to my left, calmly firing 40 mm grenades from his M203 grenade launcher into a machine-gun bunker deeper in the palm grove. I rise from a knee to a crouch and move forward into the palm grove. Then I see Evnin go down. He clutches at his gut and writhes on the ground. A corpsman appears seemingly from nowhere and is working on him. I keep moving forward into the grove. The platoon is now engaged in a hand-grenade duel at a range of 10 or 15 meters.

We are better grenade throwers than the Iraqi defenders. One basic tenet we drilled into our skulls in training is that when attacking a dug-in enemy, high explosives (HE) are what breaks positions. When assaulting a defensive position, bullets do the suppressing, but HE does the real work. We now deliver that HE from tank main guns, rockets, mortars, and grenades. The infantry surges forward behind waves of grenades and rockets to close on the enemy and finish them in their holes and bunkers with point-blank rifle fire. The enemy is now on the horns of a dilemma. If he gets up to run from his fortifications, he will be cut down by machine-gun and rifle fire; if he stays in his hole, he is ripped apart by grenades and rockets. The enemy dies both ways.

Every firefight, even one as concentrated in time and space as the fight at Al Kut, is really the sum of many smaller fights. On a field of less than six hectares, seemingly random actions now share a dynamic relationship in ways impossible to anticipate, a kaleidoscopic cause-and-effect of innumerable imponderables, accented by chance and possibly fate. Only after the firefight is over does a remotely coherent picture of the actualities of the action come into focus for those who have been a part of it.

As the infantry begins to tear the enemy out of their holes, the Red Platoon that has passed through the kill zone engages the dug-in T-62s and armored personnel carriers arrayed to support their own infantry. The 120 mm rounds of the Tigers are turning the enemy armor into geysers of flame and metal, immolating the crews inside. Two tanks in Red Platoon, under Staff Sergeant Nick Popaditch, charge off the levy road and into the eastern edge of the palm grove and close with the enemy. In a scene reminiscent of Alexander the Great's Companion Cavalry bowling over the household guard of the Persian King Darius at the battle of nearby Gaugamela in 331 B.C., the tanks wade into the midst of the enemy. Both tank commanders and their loaders lean over the sides of their tanks to fire their 9 mm pistols straight down into the fighting holes of the enemy, as the gunners rake the enemy with 7.62mm coaxial machine-gun fire. The combined horrors of a vicious infantry onslaught to their front and the nightmare of Tigers tearing into their flanks prove too much for the Iraqis. The rout is on. The Iraqis panic and bolt from the palm grove, seeking the relative safety of the city of Al Kut. A dozen try swimming the narrow canal that separates the city from the palm grove, but Red Platoon has a Tiger covering their "golden bridge" to sanctuary. The earlier ambushers now become the ambushed, cut down by machine guns in the canal. Their hoped-for escape route is now a kill zone littered with floating corpses.

"Ammo and casualty count!"

"Who's hit?"

"Where's Sergeant Mares?"
"Check that hole over there!"

Men call to one another as we transition to the next habituated battle drill, "consolidation on the objective." As the crash of explosions and clatter of small arms subside, short reports from individuals and teams relayed by shouts add up to form a picture as the platoon takes stock of its situation and begins piecing the situation together.

Twenty minutes has passed. Twenty minutes of a nearly indescribable assault on the senses and emotions, 20 minutes of supreme physical effort. It has been a roller-coaster ride between extremes; the senses, charged by adrenaline and a pounding heart, rise and fall in levels of acuity and volume. Sound is alternately deafening and muffled, the vision accentuated by a mental focus. The concussion and overpressure of tank main gun reports and the back blast of rockets rack the body, each powerful enough to kill if one is too close. Even when grenades, rockets, and mortars do not send fragments into flesh, the jarring shockwave against the body from their explosions is disorienting to the faculties. Each blast is the equivalent of a slap up side the head, a kick to the chest, or worse. The body seems at times sluggish to command, yet also moves in the face of danger as if obedient to habit. As the shooting stops, the senses equalize and return to normal. The body takes stock of the energy it expended in the crisis and exhaustion sets in.

The enemy is dead, incapacitated, or surrendering. The only sounds now are men calling one another, the soft roar and crackle of burning tanks and APCs and the pop of small-arms ammunition cooking off in the fires, punctuated by the periodic explosion of larger munitions succumbing to metal pyres. The grove is burning in places. An acrid smoke hangs in the air, a concoction of burning armor and seared human flesh mixed with cordite, urine, and sweat. This smell, unique to the modern battlefield, is unforgettable. Enemy dead lay twisted in grotesque contortions. Two Iraqis lay crumpled together in their fighting hole. A hand grenade has killed them; one had tried to pick it up and toss it out, only to have it explode in his grasp.

Making my way back out to the edge of the palm grove to the casualty collection point, I face the commander's most solemn, grim, and dreaded task: receiving the butcher's bill. We are collecting the enemy wounded and treating them as well. Bullets or HE have shattered their limbs or hideously dislocated their joints. Corporal Evnin already has been evacuated. Despite everyone's best efforts, he would die on the medical evacuation helicopter from the two gunshot wounds to his pelvis. Brian Lewis is not dead, as feared, only wounded. He has been shot through the hand without hitting bone or tendon. He refuses evacuation. I yield to his request. I need him for the coming fight in Baghdad, and besides, I know he could not bear to be separated from his men. Several Marines have minor fragmentation wounds from the grenade fight. Sergeant Mares's face is a sheet of blood, but he insists that the blood is not his. It is. His M-16A2 had been shot out of his hands when an enemy round hit the weapon held across his chest, showering his face and hands with shards of the round's copper jacket. We have three additional wounded who require evacuation. Corporal Irish has suffered a gunshot wound to the shoulder, but the ceramic plate in his body armor has stopped two other rounds that would have otherwise been fatal. Lance Corporals Osborn and Smith have received multiple grenade fragments that require evacuation, but they should fully recover. Despite their pain, and a steady stream of profanity, they are in good spirits, but angry for being hit and taken out of the fight. "We're sorry, sir," Irish apologizes for being shot. I am momentarily struck dumb. How do I respond to that comment? Why is he not angry with me for his wounding? I would later ponder what it could be, exactly, that motivated such will, such commitment and faithfulness for all to want to stay in the fight.

What factors won that firefight? How had such young men, many like Ladendorf less than a year out of high school, become such brave and effective fighters responding, automatically and ruthlessly, to a very grave situation? They had executed as if it were yet another drill, behaving as if this was routine, even normal. Classic behavioral and operant conditionings were contributors for certain.[1] But by itself, simple conditioning does not explain the iron will displayed by these men and their actions afterward. There was no evidence of euphoria. We had stopped killing and gave quarter once the enemy submitted and placed their hands in the air or were incapacitated by wounds. There was not a collapse into emotional heaps of internal conflict and sorrow. The mood afterward was all business.

Al Kut had been a test. Despite mental and physical exhaustion, sleep deprivation and uncertainty, despite the enemy's advantage of surprise and drawing first blood, we had closed with him at point-blank range and ravaged him. How had we, in a matter of minutes, routed a determined, well-prepared and entrenched enemy that enjoyed the often-decisive element of surprise? Technology was not the answer. Smart bombs and satellite intelligence held no sway in this fight. The superiority of our weapons was not the decisive factor. In a fast-paced, close-in fight such as this, advantages in expensive optics and communication equipment are worth nil. What gave us the edge over our enemy was an exquisite preparation of the mind and body that produced a will to fight, a will to win. We had not panicked; the enemy had. Under tremendous stress, our aim proved true and our actions quick and sharp. We had prepared ourselves for the ultimate test of battle, a clash of wills. We had performed simple ordinary actions under extraordinary conditions and had triumphed. We had inured ourselves to the sting of battle ever before the first shot was fired in anger.

I invite the reader to look back with me from the test at the palm grove in Iraq to the training in 29 Palms, California, where the leaders of the Third Battalion, Fourth Marines developed the minds, bodies, and spirits of our young warriors to deal with the rigors of combat—how we "battle-proofed" them.

During those hot months in the California high desert, we sought answers to many tough questions. What could be learned from the murky worlds of psychology, physiology, and philosophy to help prepare for the rigors of combat? What are the exogenous and endogenous factors that beat down a warrior's mind, body and spirit and the will to endure hardship? How exactly does one prepare to weather the storm of combat? What reasons, if any, really motivate men to "go to the sound of the guns"? What habits will give warriors the courage to reliably and resolutely close with the enemy? What expectations of unit leaders from fire team to battalion must be clearly understood and unfailingly carried out on the battlefield? What are the attributes of the responsible combat commander?

Together we earnestly attacked these questions and created a rigorous training program in response to the answers determined.

Alone, I wrestled with the role of the commander on the battlefield, the nexus of command, control, the importance of moral authority and just how to establish it. In my ruminations, coming home to roost was the imperative of self-study and methodical preparation required to command in battle. Command in combat requires a will that is harder than anything else it comes up against. It requires dedicated study into the art and science of war to become technically and tactically competent. Moreover, command in combat requires love. A commander must genuinely love his men and win their affections in return, and when the time comes, he must use that love to cause his men to willingly risk and even sacrifice their lives to accomplish the mission. Here lies the moral imperative of leadership. The leader is entrusted with the lives of his men and accepts unlimited liability for their welfare. The task of bearing such a burden requires more than passive preparation from organizational schooling and mandatory training. Such a task demands passion. Here I speak of passion in the medieval Latin sense of the word: to suffer for love. The passion of a commander is equal parts love, zeal, and a quiet wrath: love for the men, zeal for the lifelong study of the profession of arms and the behavior of men in battle, and quiet wrath to make the nightmares of our enemies come true.

PREDATORS AND PREY; BREEDING AGGRESSION

ALL THIS BE BUT A SHEEP IN A LION'S MOUTH EXCEPT THE BREED AND DISPOSITION OF THE PEOPLE BE STOUT AND WARLIKE.

—SIR FRANCIS BACON

America does not possess a warrior culture. Let us disabuse ourselves of the notion of the mythical American Warrior. To do otherwise is intellectual folly and reflects more wishful thinking and illusion than reality. Any notion of some innate warrior culture or an inherent fighting ability of Americans is an idea born in a hothouse that will wilt once exposed to the brutality of real battle. It is "but a sheep in a lion's mouth." Much has been written regarding American youth's desensitization to violence via Hollywood and video games. As true as that may be, there is no correlation between watching two-dimensional, third-party violence via some form of media, no matter how desensitized one is to the spectacle, and having the internal courage to overcome fear. What is conspicuously absent from these games and movies is the intensity of the fear for one's own life while still having the faculties to simultaneously face and kill an armed opponent within the bounds of the laws of land warfare, and also maintain one's values and humanity. The fact is that compared to most of the rest of the world, Americans are raised in a society of affluence and relative comfort, insulated from war's grim realities of deprivation and killing. Unlike warriors outside the Western world, we are not familiar with brutality. However, as put forward by noted historian and contemporary commentator Robert Kaplan in his book, *Warrior Politics: Why Leadership Demands a Pagan Ethos,* "[We will face] warriors—erratic primitives of shifting alliance, habituated to violence with no stake in civil order." [2]

Despite the American mainstream media's desensitizing daily deluge of violence, as a society we still fear interpersonal violence to our core. By the time we are adults, we have seen hundreds of killings and car crashes on the television or movie screen. Notwithstanding all this exposure to violence and our affinity for firearms, our alleged comfort with interpersonal violence is a cognitive illusion. The naked truth is that violence on the interpersonal level mortifies us. Ask yourself this question: Which do you fear more, death in a car crash or intimate death at the hands of another human? Intimate death is an act of ultimate domination; another human snuffs out your life at close range. Nothing unnerves us more. This is why we, as a culture, collectively denounce violence. Killing is still the ultimate societal taboo—the highest crime—and the fear of being killed by another is our greatest fear.

So where do our armed forces find warriors that are able to both overcome this fear and kill the enemy? Individual motivation for joining the "all recruited" force varies. I make the distinction here between "all volunteer" and "all recruited" because "volunteer" connotes an altruistic motive. While many join out of a sense of patriotism or duty, just as many join for educational benefits, to gain a marketable skill, or merely for something to do. Whatever the motivation for joining, growing up in the safe and relatively peaceful United States, none are inured to the dreadfulness of combat. Even in the one-half of 1 percent of the population that join the armed forces specifically to go in harm's way must be trained and have their dormant warrior attributes awakened by rigor and tempered by purpose. Therefore, I submit, this is not a "warrior class" we recruit.

There are two types of people on the battlefield: predators and prey. Boot camp provides the all-important foundation of instilling values, spirit, perhaps an institutional ethos, along with some basic skills. But these alone do not create a predator. Consider a lion cub. Its behavior mimics the actions of the adults. It stalks, pounces on its siblings, and engages in mock fights. The cub tries to look and act the part of the predator; yet it remains mere prey. Not until this cub matures and masters the skill of the hunt and the mental acuity to work as a team with the pride does the cub pass from prey to predator.

Our boot camps produce lion cubs. Motivated and willing, they labor under illusions of what combat is like, illusions largely put forth by Hollywood. As argued by Roy Grinker and John Spiegel in *Men Under Stress*, "Their minds are full of romanticized, Hollywood versions of their future actions in combat; colored with vague ideas of being a hero and winning ribbons and decorations for startling exploits ... an essentially unreal concept of battle." [3] However, there is a severe hazard when the expectations of combat, and one's performance on the battlefield are based on wishful thinking and fancy, dreaming of Ramboesque achievements rather than harsh, cold reality and rigorous drill. There exists the potential for catastrophic results.

UNDERSTANDING THE BATTLEFIELD

THE RISKS OF SUCH GULFS BETWEEN PRECON-CEPTION AND REALITY ARE COLOSSAL. BATTLE IS A TRAUMATIC EXPERIENCE AT THE BEST OF TIMES. BUT IF IT PRODUCES NOT ONLY ALL THE STRESSES OF NOISE AND DANGER, BUT ALSO THE DISLOCATION OF EXPECTATION, THEN THE RISKS OF FAILURE AND BREAKDOWN LOOM LARGE.

—RICHARD HOLMES, *ACTS OF WAR*

The battlefield is a dynamic environment that simply cannot be duplicated in training. That is not to say we cannot strive to understand the environment and man's behavior in order to learn how to best condition him for that environment. To prepare for war, the leadership of our battalion deliberately and systematically studied the effects of the battlefield and devised training and conditioning schemes to adapt our minds and bodies to the rigors of combat.

Five thousand years of recorded military history through the Bible and *The Iliad*, to the very first empires formed in Mesopotamia, detail the enduring nature of war and its devastating effects on men. The leadership within the battalion knew we had to come to understand and systematically come to grips with the enduring factors on the battlefield that could both adversely and positively affect the outcome.

Willpower enables men to resist and endure the corrosive effects of the battlefield. There are many factors that can grind away at the will of a warrior. It is each man's will that enables him to endure the effects of the battlefield and overcome both his fear of interpersonal violence and his resistance to killing. This will is transitory, expendable. In his book *On Killing*, Dr. David Grossman describes the concept of a reservoir of will as the "well of fortitude," in which resides all of a man's ability to endure the shock, horror, and hardships of combat. To illustrate, Grossman cites an anecdote recounted by Lord Moran.

> Sergeant Taylor ... was wounded and came back unchanged; he seemed proof against the accidents of his life, he stood in the Company like a rock. ... He finally suffered a near miss from an artillery shell. When Sergeant Taylor went to the well it was empty, and this indomitable rock shattered: completely and catastrophically. [4]

When a man has drawn from the "well of fortitude" too often without replenishing its stores, he runs the risk of coming up dry. And if he does he may no longer be able to overcome the base fear of killing and being killed.

What factors comprise the well of fortitude? What factors cause us to draw from the well, and what factors allow us to replenish the well?

Colonel John Allen, USMC introduced Table 1 in a lecture to the students and faculty of the Marine Corps Amphibious Warfare School. The table exactly illustrates factors that cause us to withdraw from and to replenish the well. Simply put, the elements under the column of "Transitory" are the factors on the battlefield, be they exogenous (external) or endogenous (internal). To endure the hardships of fear, sleeplessness, hunger, and uncertainty, withdrawals must be made from our reservoir of will, our "well of fortitude." Factors like discipline, cohesion, training, and comradeship replenish our will and restore our well of fortitude.

Table 1
The Human Factors in Battle

	Transitory (Withdrawals/Debits)	Enduring (Replenishment/Credits)
Endogenous	- confinement - cowardliness - emotion - energy - fear - isolation - mental fatigue - physical fatigue - sleep loss - stress - surprise - uncertainty	- cognitive factors - cohesion - combat experience - comradeship - discipline - honor - initiative - intuition - leadership - morale - national characteristics - social motivation - training/experience - will/motivation
Exogenous	- weather conditions - visibility - darkness - fire - noise - soldiers load	- toxicity (NBC) - terrain - coordination

Source: John Allen, "Human Factors in Combat," lecture delivered to the Marine Corps Amphibious Warfare School, Quantico, VA, 18 August 2001

Within the battalion we approached this challenge in several ways—psychologically, philosophically, and physiologically. First came classic behavioral conditioning designed to create the *unshakeable habits* that could provide nearly automatic responses to battle situations. The battle drills we executed in the Al Kut firefight were to become for us a classic case in point.

Next came physical conditioning, cognitive training, and operant conditioning to, as much as possible in the training setting, prepare our bodies and minds to recognize and accept the stress of combat, the seeming chaos of combat, as being normal, thus preventing what Richard Holmes calls "dislocation of expectation." In another lecture at the Marine Corps Amphibious Warfare School, Dr. David Grossman likened the transitory and endogenous effects of the battlefield, the corrosive factors, to a "virus" that can be resisted through systematic "inoculations." [5] Just as we medically inoculate ourselves against diseases by introducing a small dose of the pathogen to the body, the same holds true for the viruses of fear, exhaustion, uncertainty, and sleep deprivation. In short, we would be giving ourselves "inoculations" to the viruses of combat.

Our final preparation dealt with the act of killing, the essence of war. Our challenge was to prepare our young warriors to kill legitimate human targets without hesitation, to understand when the killing had to stop, and to control the inclination to feel guilty for killing once the fighting ended. Much like professional athletes mentally imaging themselves performing in competition, we actively imaged our Marines and Sailors in the act of killing the enemy, of ourselves being wounded by the enemy, of our fellow warriors being killed and wounded, and our reactions through a dozen other scenarios. This was not an exercise in delusions of grandeur; in fact, it was just the opposite. Imaging must be coupled closely with the habits formed in behavioral training, as well as the physical and mental inoculations administered. We then turned to hardening our minds, bodies, and spirits by developing the Five Battlefield Habits.

THE FIVE HABITS AND THE COURAGE TO CLOSE WITH THE ENEMY

HABIT HARDENS THE BODY FOR GREAT EXERTIONS, STRENGTHENS THE HEART IN GREAT PERIL, AND FORTIFIES THE JUDGMENT AGAINST FIRST IMPRESSIONS. HABIT BREEDS THAT PRICELESS QUALITY, CALM, WHICH, PASSING FROM HUSSAR AND RIFLEMAN UP TO THE TO THE GENERAL HIMSELF, WILL LIGHTEN THE COMMANDER'S TASK.

—CARL VON CLAUSEWITZ, *ON WAR*

Task Force, 3rd Battalion, 4th Marines took Clausewitz's insight quoted above as the very foundation of its training plan. We focused on the principle of habit in five basic areas where we wanted flawless performance: combat marksmanship, combat conditioning, casualty evacuation, specific battle drills, and discipline—habits to be ingrained so thoroughly that our Marines would be able to fight, win, and survive at least the first five days of combat. After the first five days, we felt that they would have seen enough of combat to be able to avoid death from simple mistakes from then on. From these ingrained habits would flow confidence, aggressiveness, a bias for action, and, most of all, the courage to close with and kill the enemy.

Habit One: Combat Marksmanship

In the whole of the initial assault on the Omaha Beachhead, there were only about five infantry companies which were tactically effective. ... At their backs was the power of the mightiest sea and air forces ever to support an invading army in the history of the world. But in the hour of crisis for these infantry companies, the metal, guns and bombs of these distant supporters were not worth three squads from that small band of men which had gone to work with their grenades and rifles.

—S.L.A. Marshall, *Men Against Fire*

Combat Marksmanship is the hallmark of the infantryman. Nothing nurtures confidence quite like the knowledge that one can hit what one is shooting at, and that his buddies also can hit that at which they aim. Anybody, even in the middle of a phobic response to the violence of combat, can yank on a trigger and spray rounds in the general direction of the enemy, to "spray and pray." In training we drilled combat marksmanship under the most realistic conditions that we could muster. Our standard was to employ our weapons quickly and with a high degree of accuracy. We conducted all marksmanship training according to the following six commandments:

The Six Commandments of Combat Marksmanship Training

1. **You shall wear 100 percent of your combat kit (helmet, flak, ammo, water, load bearing equipment [40–60 lbs].**

2. **All firing shall have target feedback mechanisms (the more immediate the feedback the better: balloons, bowling pins, etc.).**

3. **All firing shall be associated with a standard of performance for every round (percent of hits per rounds fired, distribution of rounds on targets, etc.).**

4. **All training tasks shall be conducted under increasingly realistic conditions both day and night, with nuclear, biological, and chemical (NBC) suits on and under physical duress.**

5. **Targetry shall replicate battlefield conditions such as array and exposure (targets matched to terrain, exposure of targets in terms of amount visible and for duration of time visible).**

6. **All weapons shall be integrated to include grenades, in all live-fire training (stack tasks, fire and movement to gain a position of advantage, and employment of rockets or grenades—no exceptions).**

Al Kut and every other firefight the battalion lived through in Iraq validated these commandments. During the march to Baghdad, retired Marine Major General Ray "E-Tool" Smith, a highly decorated Vietnam veteran and a boyhood hero of mine, accompanied our task force for several days. He strongly commended the battalion's combat marksmanship.

When fighting at Al Kut, we were not neatly arrayed along a grassy firing line, with shooting gloves and jackets, engaging fully exposed paper targets at known distances. We wore chemical suits and body armor, with ungainly helmets bouncing around on our heads and rivulets of sweat stinging our eyes. Our training systematically had habituated the battalion to the chaotic environment we found in the palm grove and every other subsequent fight. The negative factors of the battlefield—fear, dust, heat, noise, confusion, the weight of our combat gear, and the uncertainty of the enemy disposition—were to an extent all normal to us. We had largely neutralized the impact of these factors through hard, realistic training.

Our targets were not pristine silhouettes but partial forms of human heads and shoulders—forms that were actively doing their best to kill us. More often than not, we could not clearly see the enemy and simply fired at the muzzle flashes. Our training taught Marines to expect small, elusive targets and to effectively engage them while at the same time searching out enemy positions that could provide support to the ones we were trying to overrun. We arrayed our targets per enemy doctrine, and we always provided target arrays that simulated an enemy counterattack.

The sixth commandment—integration of all weapons systems—paid off handsomely during the violent harmony of the palm grove at Al Kut. Our operations officer, Major Martin Wetterauer, had been a squad leader in a reserve Marine infantry battalion in Operation Desert Storm in 1991. He told of a fight his platoon had with an entrenched enemy unit of six men. He described how the firefight that should have been over in a few minutes lasted more than an hour because it was fought only with rifles and the M249 SAW (squad automatic weapon). Even though Wetterauer's unit had rockets, hand grenades, and M203 grenade launchers, they were never employed in that fight because they were forgot in the heat of battle because integration of weapons had not been drilled. Had the HE been employed, the fight would have been over quickly.

We trained our riflemen to maneuver forward to a "position of advantage," that position from which we could place the fullest array of HE in our arsenal on the enemy. Over and over again we practiced "lane training," where buddy teams would advance by alternate bounds while engaging the enemy, one prepared to shoot while the other moved. This drill was the "bread and butter" enabler of nearly every firefight—and we drilled to very high standards of speed of movement, selection of terrain, and accuracy of fires, and, above all, of never making an uncovered move. The standard was always high regardless of the conditions. We often drilled marksmanship tasks competitively at the end of a week of punishing field exercises in 115-degree heat.

Every Marine was required to be qualified with his weapon, not just on the normal qualification course but on advanced combat courses, often designed by our own officers and noncommissioned officers. The rule for these courses was to replicate anticipated combat conditions wherever reasonably possible. Even a weapon as simple and intuitive as a hand grenade was not issued until an individual had demonstrated proficiency by throwing for accuracy and time from various positions: prone, kneeling and standing, at varying ranges, and at target arrays. The result: at Al Kut our grenades went right into the enemy's holes, trenches, and bunker apertures. Our warriors reflexively knew how to kill; they were supremely confident in their ability to "make the enemy fall down." In the palm grove, our training sustained us. We were "scary good" at applying violence in a very precise manner to kill the enemy and preserve our own lives.

Habit Two: Combat Conditioning

Truly then, it is killing men with kindness not to insist upon physical standards during training which will give them a maximum fitness for the extraordinary stress of campaigning in war.

—S. L. A. Marshall. *Men Against Fire*

The second habit was combat conditioning. Our physical training did not involve running in sneakers and nylon shorts, or getting buffed beach muscles in the gym. Our conditioning focused on preparing for the rigors of combat. These included long foot marches under heavy loads, martial arts, grappling, and physical conditioning with combat equipment on. We trained our task force as though the men were professional athletes. We provided classes on nutrition, given by the base hospital's dietician, and state-of-the-art functional weight training and cardiovascular fitness.

In the National Football League, injured players are rehabilitated methodically. They suit up and play hurt every Sunday. Far too often, injured or weaker Marines are cast aside as flotsam and jetsam and allowed to become non-participatory burdens to the unit. We systematically ensured that those who lagged or were injured consulted with the resident experts (dieticians, physical therapists, and medical officers) to develop a "get-well plan" that would be supervised by the individual's unit leaders. We ensured that every Marine and Sailor suited up and remained a contributing member of the team.

Our combat training also was persistently carried out under every "debit" condition we could muster realistically. We employed classic operant conditioning—conditioning Marines to behave in ways to exert influence and control over their environment, no matter how challenging.

Another valuable training strategy was the development of a competition coined the "Darkside Derby" that was designed to give the unit a "game day" to aim for. We set a date four months out and published the events of the competition. We designed the events to develop and test all-around physical fitness for the Marines and Sailors. A full week was set aside for the derby, in which each squad was to compete for standing. Day One would be the standard Marine Corps Physical Fitness Test (PFT), consisting of a three-mile run, pull-ups, and sit-ups. Day Two would be weightlifting, requiring every Marine to bench press his body weight 10 times, squat his body weight 10 times, and dead lift his body weight 10 times. The goal was to foster core-strength development, crucial for carrying a fighting load in combat, as well as to educate everyone on proper weight training. Day Three was a 10-mile run. Day Four was the obstacle course in full combat kit. Day Five was a 20-mile forced march for time up the nearly 11,000-foot Mount San Jacinto.

The genius of the program was that it was a competition, and Marines naturally are competitive. The squads used spare time to train on their own. Nobody wanted to be embarrassed. The other benefit was that the "gym-rats" had to hit the road, and the "greyhound" runners had to hit the weights. Sadly, the derby had to be cancelled when the battalion's deployment date was moved up. We were disappointed, but we still had gained all the benefits of the program.

The importance of such training cannot be overstated. Severe physical fatigue makes an individual vulnerable to a wide array of afflictions. Napoleon's linking of fatigue with cowardice is as valid as it is potent: The connection between physical fatigue and psychiatric breakdown in battle is well known.

Habit Three: Casualty Evacuation

There was … a frank recognition that aggression could only be maintained if soldiers knew that they would be well looked after if they were wounded.
—Richard Holmes, *Acts of War*

Just as marksmanship engenders confidence, so does the knowledge that if one is struck down in the fight one will be treated and evacuated promptly and professionally. On the very first foot march I conducted as the battalion commander back in 29 Palms, California, we suffered a heat casualty. This event was a critical indicator of just how badly prepared to handle casualties we were. A young man went down during a halt very early in the hike. By the time I made my way back to his location at the rear of the column, I had expected that he would have been treated already and in the process of evacuation. When I arrived, I was witness to what seemed like an episode of *The Jerry Springer Show*: all drama and no progress. The afflicted Marine was semi-conscious and limp as a rag doll, as I watched our young and inexperienced corpsmen completely botch the first-aid procedures for heat injury and the evacuation. The battalion sergeant major soon took over and sorted it all out. The Marine turned out to be fine, though badly dehydrated. He was the victim of both poor small-unit leadership that never monitored his hydration and the complete lack of proficiency of our medical personnel.

However, the real damage was done to the confidence of his mates who witnessed the debacle. The unspoken thought in all of our minds was, "I hope if I'm hit, these jokers don't show up to help. I'll take my chances." Such an attitude is poison in a unit and can create animosity between the corpsmen of the battalion aid station and the rest of the unit. Such a spectacle never was allowed again.

The battalion embarked on a systematic training program to handle casualties from the point of injury, to the battalion aid station, and on to further medical treatment. Every man received additional training to care for his own wounds and those of his buddies. We also selected men from every squad to receive advanced lifesaving training in the event that the corpsman was a casualty himself or was overwhelmed. Our corpsmen were drilled to standard repeatedly. They even took turns spending nights at various trauma centers in Los Angeles to help inoculate them to the spectacle of gore and learn from the positive example of cool professional responding to emergencies.

Just as we did in our marksmanship training, we rehearsed the care and evacuation of our wounded under all conditions and types of wounds. We engendered confidence by training all hands to handle any injury under fire, whether it was day, night, or under nuclear, biological, and chemical conditions. Furthermore, the energy and concern put forward by the leadership of the task force eased the mind of the families and strengthened the bonds of trust between the leaders and led.

The results were priceless. Our corpsmen and task-force surgeons were superb in combat and were recognized as the best-trained medical personnel in the regiment by the regimental surgeon. A deep mutual respect was developed between the corpsmen and the Marines as each committed to taking care of the other. This mutual dependence is indispensable on the battlefield. It is a force multiplier that reduces the battlefield's "debit" factors of uncertainty, fear, and isolation and replaces them with the will-sustaining "credit" factors of cohesion, confidence, and comradeship.

Habit Four: Battle Drills

Part of the stress of battle stems from its puzzling and capricious nature: battle drills help minimize the randomness of battle and give the soldier familiar points of contact in an uncertain environment, like lighthouses in a stormy sea.
—Richard Holmes, *Acts of War*

G-Day, 21 March 2003. Our task force is attacking against the Iraqi 31st Mechanized Infantry Brigade, when a section of the 81 mm mortar platoon moving in direct support of Kilo Company comes under machine-gun and RPG fire from an enemy position 300 meters to the left flank. The mortar platoon commander, First Lieutenant Matt Danner, has drilled his platoon to these "hip shoots"; it is second nature to them. Despite heavy and accurate enemy fire, the Marines dismount their vehicles, moving with the precision of a machine. In a few seconds, the platoon will have a dozen or so 10-pound 81 mm high-explosive mortar rounds in the air and on trajectory to kill the enemy. But it is not that simple in combat. The column is traveling on a raised levy road as it comes under fire. The platoon moves to seek the defilade cover provided by the depression to the right of the road. Staff Sergeant Justice, the section leader, directs the section to use the "direct alignment" method of fire. Direct alignment is a rapid and accurate technique that allows the mortar crews to take advantage of the mortar's high angle of fire by firing from a covered position, protected from the enemy's direct fires. The crew puts a red-and-white striped direction stake (a "candy cane" without the curved top) exactly on line between the enemy position and the mortar tubes in defilade. This stake serves the purpose of providing an artificial aim point. By aiming at the stake "on top of the terrain," the tubes can be aligned on the enemy position from a position of defilade. The crew simply estimates the range to the target and then places rounds on the enemy without exposing itself to direct return fire. The crew makes subsequent corrections to deflection by adjusting their aim on the direction stake. This "hip shoot" battle drill requires the ammo man to expose himself to the enemy long enough to sink the aiming stake the prescribed 50-meter distance from the mortar firing line. The ammo man is PFC Travis Bennett, and he is in the very first firefight of his life. Bennett runs through enemy fire to sink the stake as he has done in a thousand drills. But this time the necessary position for the stake is on an asphalt road! Despite this being his debut firefight, he is undeterred by either the small-arms impacts around him or the asphalt that is preventing him from sinking the stake. But a battle drill is a battle drill. Bennett lays prone in the road, fully exposed to enemy fire, holding the aiming stake steady with one hand while covering his eyes with the other to fend off the asphalt being kicked up by the enemy bullets. Everyone is stunned at his solution. With a shake of the head and few gallows humor "cat-calls" of good-natured ribbing aimed at Bennett, the mortar section is soon on target, and the enemy is killed.

Despite our best efforts to replicate combat, our peacetime battle drills never can match the complexity, confusion, and fear of the real thing. Bennett's "solution" wasn't taught, but the urgency of the situation called for just that solution. Without the "lighthouse" of battle drill, the platoon could not have performed as well it did that day and every day thereafter, leaving improvisation to small details and nuance, not mission-essential tasks.

As task-force leaders, we deliberately set about forecasting what we believed would be the most crucial battle drills, then rehearsed those drills hundreds of times under increasingly challenging conditions. There was no magic to the drills; for the most part they were the same rehearsed by any other unit. The difference, if any, was the number of times we repeated them, the increasing difficulty of the conditions under which we did them, and the way we coached or "imaged" the Marines through them. Again, the idea was to provide a sense that the chaos surrounding the individual and unit in combat was quite normal, and, as such, "things were as they could be expected to be."

One key element that gave Lieutenant Colonel Phil Skuta, Commanding Officer of 2nd Battalion, 7th Marines, RCT-7 for Operation Iraqi Freedom 2, his peace of mind was the knowledge that he was employing his men in accordance with their capabilities. "Employing a command according to its capabilities was vital to achieving success. Commanders and leaders that do not give the time to understand individual and collective capabilities may unknowingly assign missions with little chance of success." [6] Only by rigorous training held to an unyielding standard can a commander truly assess the individual and collective capabilities of his men. Skuta further explains that, since his battalion did not participate in Operation Iraqi Freedom 1 and lacked the benefit of combat experience the employment of strict standards developed in training gives a commander concrete information on the true capabilities of his subordinate units and provided the foundation for his mental risk assessment to any mission assigned. Using training standards was an indispensable yardstick for assessing risk and assigning missions. In 3rd Battalion, 4th Marines we developed our own advanced certification course for HMMWV drivers we dubbed the "Rough Rider Course." To qualify, each driver during the course of a week drove the vehicle across varied terrain that often approached the limits of the vehicle in terms of slope gradient and negotiating ditches. The driver was required to negotiate several routes both as a single vehicle, and as a member of a convoy, under day and night conditions as well as recover a stuck vehicle. As a commander planning a cross desert night movement to conduct a raid on an insurgent position in western Iraq, the knowledge that all drivers were "Rough Rider" qualified gave me a sense that a 60-mile cross-country movement across very dissected terrain on a route we never had traversed, on a particularly dark night, was well within the art of the possible because we had trained to standard.

Battle drills—the physical acts of responding to a situation, be it "contact right," call for fire, a hip shoot, putting a rocket shot or grenade into an enemy bunker— were carefully linked with mental imaging. These images were not foolish delusions of grandeur; we did our best to conjure up the fear and confusion of the battlefield, and mentally associated the emotions with the situation calling for a particular battle drill. We dealt with the emotions of killing, comrades being killed or grievously wounded, or ourselves being wounded, and linked them to the actions that would have to take place in those situations on the field of combat.

The battle drill of "contact right" used in the Al Kut firefight had been rehearsed and imaged dozens of times before Al Kut became part of our lexicon and unit history. We imaged riding buttoned up in the AAVs, the deafening roar of the diesel engines, the smell of the exhaust, the pervasive rhythmic jostling and churning of the tracks. We imaged the sound of enemy fire, the deafening report of our vehicles' up-gun weapons returning fire, Mk-19 grenade launchers or M2 .50 caliber machine guns barking, and brass tinkling onto the hull.

A Marine yelling six inches from your face relays the call of "contact right," but you barely can hear him. The vehicle slams to a halt, throwing you forward into your buddy, the ramp drops, and you rush forward into the light, following the man in front of you. You can't see the enemy! Your heart is in your throat. Rounds whine, thump and ping as they impact all around you. You see your fire-team leader pointing at a bunker. You turn to your buddy, and together you begin to fire and move together. You pick out the muzzle flashes of the enemy. You cover your buddy as he moves. You see a small fold in the ground, and as soon as your buddy is firing, you move to it, chanting the cadence of "I'm up; he sees me; I'm down." You know you need to get HE on the bunker because HE breaks positions. You reach for a fragmentation grenade; you do not have to look for it because it is where it has always been. Your body is on automatic pilot. You yell "frag out" per the battle drill and throw from the prone at the bunker aperture. Your aim is true; the bunker is silenced. In the Al Kut palm grove, PFC Dusty Ladendorf did not suffer from the dislocation of expectation that causes men to freeze; he knew what to expect and he knew how to react. He expected fear, confusion, and uncertainty, not just in an intellectual or academic sense, but viscerally. At Al Kut he linked and internalized the emotional and physical, and he performed flawlessly in the most dire of situations. He was a hero that day.

How will a Marine handle the spectacle of his buddy going down in a firefight? The battle drills told us to keep moving toward the enemy, confidant that the corpsmen would tend our wounded. Killing the enemy would be the best way to help our fallen. On paper this is obvious, but in practice one must override the nearly overwhelming emotions and impulses to go to the wounded. Linking the emotions to the battle drill was of inestimable value. We imaged ourselves through our own wounding, real wounds, such as traumatic amputations or seeing our own blood and intestines spilling on the ground. Keeping one's head could be life saving. Imaging through the emotions of seeing limbs smashed and linking those emotions to the physical battle drill of applying self-aid with a battle dressing or tourniquet is a good way to produce the desired behavior when it counts.

We did the same with radio reports. Information is like gold in combat; clear, concise reporting in a calm, steady voice is the irreducible bottom line. We not only repeatedly drilled our unit leaders on reporting, but we drilled them over the map board of our G-Day objectives. We practiced reporting the most likely situations we would experience—for example, enemy contact, and requests for fire, position reports, and medical evacuations. By using the coordinates of our intended objectives and where we thought we would likely encounter the enemy, we were able to internalize our plans and every possible variation to those plans we could think of. We added realism by delivering our reports over actual radios. This may sound absurdly simple, but no one is immune to the "abadaba disease" in which one's speech turns to mush the second the handset is keyed.

On the night of our first day in combat, the task force was on the outskirts of Al Basra. At one point all three of the line companies were in contact, the two combined-arms anti-armor teams (CAATs) were in contact, and enemy mortar rounds were landing on the task force command post and combat trains. The battalion was in contact with the enemy everywhere. You never would have known it by listening to the radio. One battalion watch officer remarked afterward, "It sounded just like we're back on the map board rehearsing again." Officers under fire almost casually gave reports on enemy contacts in a clipped, rhythmic cadence. Only the sound of gunfire in the background betrayed the fact that this was for real. Why? We had been there before in our training and rehearsals. I am convinced that had we not practiced and drilled to the extent we did, more mistakes would have been committed, and we would have generated much more drama and confusion than was necessary—and more casualties would have been suffered.

Habit Five: Discipline

> *True military discipline extends not from knowledge, but habit.*
>
> —General Hans von Seeckt

When the 1st Marine Division began preparations for deployment to Kuwait for what would later be known as Operation Iraqi Freedom (OIF), our Commanding General, Major General J. M. Mattis, gathered his battalion commanders and described his vision of success. Part of that vision was being "brilliant at the basics." He went on to emphasize the inherent difficulties, but that mastery of the basics was all it would take to whip anybody. As I contemplated "the basics," I began to write them down in bullet format. I realized that at the root of being brilliant at the basics was *habituated discipline*. Discipline is not necessarily instant obedience to orders. Nor is it punishment to correct deficiencies. Rather, discipline is reinforced habit designed to produce a specific character, or pattern of behavior, that is strong enough to override creature comforts, personal wants, and lapses in fortitude. In short, the habituated discipline we sought was a form of amicable discipline and self-control, a code of behavior, generated from within.

I wanted to produce a document that was so succinct that there could be no room for misunderstanding even by the youngest Marine or Sailor on his first day in the battalion. Nevertheless, my primary audience was leaders—the lieutenants, staff noncommissioned officers and noncommissioned officers, the backbone of the battalion. What follows is that document, entitled *Expectations of Combat Leaders*. I personally briefed it to every noncommissioned officer and above, and we internalized the basics through training and ruthless enforcement of standards. We made those basics *habit*. Even then, we experienced letdowns. Each leader was challenged to honestly ask himself how well his unit was doing and then repeatedly ask himself, "How do we do better?"

Expectations of Combat Leaders is filled with the wisdom of those who have gone before, wisdom that has been written in blood by generations of warriors. Many of the "bullets" have been provided by Major General James N. Mattis, and others have been provided by Marines with whom I have served or by great historical figures such as General John A. Lejuene, General Matthew B. Ridgway, Field Marshal Erwin Rommel, and Major General Carl von Clausewitz. This document served us well in combat. The firefight in the palm grove outside Al Kut was a manifestation of it.

EXPECTATIONS OF COMBAT LEADERS

Leadership

- As Leaders, you are the standard-bearers of our Corps' history, reputation, and values. Marines and Sailors will look to you for their cues. Everything you do or say, or fail to do or say, will set the tone for your unit. You are *always* in charge. Creature comforts are secondary elements of troop welfare. First-rate training, dedicated leadership, and a sense of belonging to a tight unit are true troop welfare. Only when the latter is missing does the former take on importance.
- *Encourage constructive feedback.* Continue to use the after-action review (AAR) as a means for this, especially in combat. Our best ideas and tactics, techniques, and procedures (TTPs) will come from our NCOs and junior Marines.

Sometimes leadership means making people do what they know deep down they should be doing anyway. It often means being unpopular. Marines need a leader, not a buddy. Making the "easy" or popular decision, instead of the difficult and unpopular but correct decision, will reward you with mission failure and make casualties of your Marines.

General John A. Lejeune has wisely stated, "Leaders must have a strong sense of the great responsibility of their office; the resources they expend in war are human lives." Remember, the *enemy*, not an inspection team, will grade us on our capabilities.

Treat our Marines and Sailors with respect. They are willing to execute your orders and die doing so. *Lead,* don't push, them up that hill. Get negative with a Marine as a last resort.

Stop rumors immediately.

As a unit, we must be in harmony. Trust your chain of command. Once a decision is made, support it 100 percent. Never do anything that fosters the notion: "Higher up is screwed up." Remember, *you* are somebody's "higher up."

Be Brilliant at the Basics, the Basics will be Habit

Carl von Clausewitz stated, "Habit hardens the body for great exertions, strengthens the heart in great peril. Habit breeds that priceless quality, *calm,* which, passing from rifleman to commander will lighten the task." [7]

- Great units do the basics with a high degree of proficiency and as habit. *Good habits breed smart, tough, aggressive Marines and Sailors that will win in combat. Bad habits breed timidity. Timidity breeds casualties and mission failure.*

Training

- *Everything is training. Never miss an opportunity to train.* Training does *not* stop in theater. Make a list of your unit tasks and battle drills that you are most dissatisfied with and use that as your start point for "opportunity training." This type of training usually comprises most of your small-unit training time. Accept the fact that you will not be popular when you force your unit to drill the basics, but you will be keeping them alive. *Focus on the basics and become brilliant at them.*

Physical Training

- Physical Training is conducted daily in accordance with the situation. Life in a combat zone will present very few opportunities for formation physical training (PT) above the platoon level, yet we must maintain our conditioning. At a minimum, a 15-minute combination of stretching, calisthenics, rifle PT, isometric and resistance exercises, and martial arts will suffice for maintenance of conditioning. This sharpens the mind and warms the body. Develop a program and couple it with your monitored hygiene program; that is, PT followed by monitored hygiene and laundry and weapons maintenance.

Combat Marksmanship

- This is our reason for being. Nothing will give a Marine more confidence to close with the enemy than the knowledge that he and his fellow Marines will hit what they shoot at. You must enforce great battle sight zero (BZO) data that is verified periodically to include PEQ-2s (laser aiming devices). You must ensure that you are getting target feedback and applying it to a *standard*.
- Conduct drills on Condition 1 reloads/reload drills. This must be routine and accomplished blindfolded and on the run. This will save lives one day. Immediate and remedial actions in response to weapon malfunctions are vital and must be performed blindfolded as well.

Weapons:

- Ensure weapons and ammo are cleaned and inspected at every opportunity. Do not allow slings to be removed from weapons or employed other than loop to swivel. The sling is there for a reason. When wrapped around the carrying handle, it impedes one's sight picture and negates the use of a hasty sling. Allowing Marines to carry a weapon that cannot be properly employed is a leadership failure.

- *Weapons Maintenance:* Most malfunctions and stoppages are self-induced by the shooter. Poor reloading and dirty weapons are usually the reason, and this is overcome by NCOs doing their jobs. Before and after every action, NCOs will ensure weapons are in the proper condition code, cleaned, lubricated, and with Battle Site Zero set on the rear sight. Ammo is checked, and grenades are inspected. Broken and malfunctioning weapons will be reported immediately. *Before doing anything else (eating, sleeping, etc.), weapons will be cleaned and ready.*

Discipline

- Do not allow graffiti on uniforms, do-rags, wristbands, or other forms of jackassery, period.
- Pre-Combat Checks and Inspections and Post-Combat Checks and Inspections are SOP and are at the *very heart* of leadership. This is a *basic habit.* They are called Pre-Combat Checks and Inspections for a reason; they are *not* Pre-Combat questions and assumptions. Leaders at the squad level carry out Checks and Inspections; platoon commanders and platoon sergeants verify—*no exceptions._*
- *Prescribed Load:* Allow no deviations from the prescribed load and basic uniform—*ever.* Deviations are conscious decisions by a commanding officer based on analysis of the situation, *not* personal whims. At a minimum, Marines and Sailors will have their gas mask and weapons on their bodies *at all times.*
- Helmets, when worn, will have the chinstrap on the chin; otherwise, it will not stay on when needed most. Allowing a Marine to wear the helmet without a chinstrap is making the Marine wear useless weight on his head and is a leadership failure.
- *Communications discipline:* Enforce proper reporting and communications procedures. Use of "pro-words" (standardized radio jargon), reporting formats, and proper radio checks cut down on traffic and confusion.
- *Light discipline:* Will be strictly enforced. Use of flashlights in the open, smoking and vehicle headlights from dusk to dawn is a commanding officer's decision, not one of personal convenience. We have Night Vision Devices (NVDs); use them. There is seldom a reason to break light discipline.
- *Hygiene discipline:* Disease will cause casualties and rob units of combat power faster than the enemy could ever hope to do. Prior to eating chow in the field, squad leaders will inspect their squads for proper hygiene, clean hands, clean weapons, and the prescribed uniforms. Poor hygiene will rob us of combat power. All Marines and Sailors will perform hygiene every day, shaving and brushing teeth at a minimum, with periodic foot inspections by leaders. Hand washing is mandatory and monitored. Leaders at the squad level check; platoon commanders and platoon sergeants verify—*no exceptions.*

Security

- Security is a habit formed at home; otherwise it will be an afterthought, and we will suffer for it. I expect you to be naturally curious about your surroundings— you are always on patrol. Never abdicate the security of your unit to anyone else.
- Never send Marines or Sailors alone anywhere. Everything is done in buddy teams, even head calls. *This fundamental will not be violated.*
- Security is 360 degrees; from buddy team to battalion, we will have 360-degree security. Be a hard target.

Contact with the Enemy

- We are a combat unit that is *expert in the application of violence.* Trust your instincts and make a decision in accordance with your higher's intent. I will support you. Use combat patience, suppress the enemy, and when you move, do it with purpose, aggression, and violence of action intent on finishing the enemy.
- After first contact, the enemy will fear us more than they hate us.
- Never make an "uncovered move" in the face of the enemy. From buddy rushes to bounding by platoons, always have an overwatch element prepared to deliver fires.
- We will take casualties in combat; men will die. Accept that as fact now, and resolve to stay above the emotion and remain focused on the mission. Do not allow casualties to slow our speed. The best way to take care of our wounded is to finish the enemy off.
- Treat the dead, friendly and enemy, with respect. Do not pose for photos with the enemy dead or otherwise desecrate their remains; it is cowardly.
- Upon contact with the enemy, establish *violence supremacy* and kill them. If they quit, then give quarter. Keep our honor clean; do not allow atrocities that will sully our reputation, make cowards of our Marines, and stiffen the enemy's resolve.
- Treat prisoners with dignity, but do not trust them; be forceful and firm. Do not abuse prisoners; it is cowardly.
- Treat the locals with dignity and be courteous, but never be "friendly." It is a weakness they will exploit.
- Dedicate yourself to the unit and mission. Trust in your brothers. Make peace with your maker, then fight with a "happy heart."

On the surface, these expectations look simple to the point of being a blinding flash of the obvious. That is true; there are no great revelations. But that is the elusiveness of habituated discipline. The basics are easy to talk about but hard to maintain. They require vigilant, iron-willed leaders who maintain an unflinching standard day in and day out despite fatigue, boredom, and complacency. I found we had to hit the "reset button" every 10 days or so. Just before redeployment back home, when it was 130 degrees, we had to "reset" every seven days. By "reset button," I mean we conducted training and inspections that reinforced and reemphasized the basics to include demonstrating weapons-handling procedures, confirming battle-sight-zero, basic fighting loads, battle drills, and so on. That act was not only necessary for the men to reinforce habituated actions, but, more importantly, it reminded leaders, myself included, to "be deaf to expediency" and do the right thing even though we were tired, hot, or lazy. On a more philosophical level, the expectations of combat leaders were simple basics held to an impeccable standard. Once achieved, the unit achieved virtuosity, or simply, performed common tasks with uncommon proficiency. The challenge for you—the leader—is to internalize these expectations in your unit, to ingrain them so fully that they are habit, lest you be taught a bitter lesson.

This approach to a written list of expectations was not unique to 3/4. LTC Harry Tunnell IV, U.S. Army was the commanding officer of 1st Battalion (Airborne), 508th Infantry, 173rd Airborne Brigade. During the opening stages of Operation Iraqi Freedom Tunnell made the jump with his battalion and led it through eight months of combat operations before being seriously wounded and evacuated from the theater. LTC Tunnell was adamant that the reason for the success of his unit in combat, while keeping casualties as low as possible, was strict adherence to standards and discipline. In Tunnell's words, "Define standards, train people on what they are, and enforce them. It is not a standard until it is written and understood. Your unit will fight the way they have trained regardless of whether you want them to or not." [8] Tunnell illustrated his point by describing an action in which a support platoon conducting a daylight resupply convoy was ambushed. "The ambush was Initiated by with a daisy chain of several improvised explosive devices (IEDs) wounding 2 soldiers driving a fuel truck. The enemy followed up the IEDs with rocket-propelled grenades medium machineguns and AK-47s." [9] The platoon responded exactly as it was trained. The large resupply vehicles raced out of the kill zone and rallied at a preplanned point while the convoy commander called in a contact report that set in motion the movement of reinforcements, casualty evacuation assets, and Apache Longbow attack helicopters. "The final and most critical part of the platoon's set procedure was for the escorting vehicles and any other vehicles carrying troops to turn into the ambush and dismount the paratroopers to fight. By the time the reinforcing elements arrived the support platoon had killed or captured all the attackers." [10] In a post-engagement conversation with a senior officer, Tunnell was flabbergasted when this senior officer suggested that the reason for the platoon's success was that they were just "physically tougher" than the enemy. Tunnell admitted that while physical fitness was an element of the convoy's success, the real seeds of victory were found in the exacting standards and discipline enforced by small-unit leaders who bore detailed rehearsals and pre-combat checks and inspections. In short, the platoon behaved in combat exactly the way they had been trained.

Throughout training and deployment, the leadership of the 3rd Battalion, 4th Marines placed a premium on poise. Our mantra was to "act as if you've been there before." That one phrase set the tone for how we would conduct ourselves before, during, and after battle. On the day we flew out from March Air Force Base to Kuwait, the Marines of Kilo Company were formed up, waiting to embark. There was not a hint of boisterousness, horseplay or overplayed bravado. When those acts are present, they are symptoms of fear and uncertainty and amount to posturing. The battalion sergeant major and I stood and observed. Kilo Company stood poised, quietly talking to each other, equipment worn correctly, and faces expressionless, as if they had done this a dozen times already. Actually, they had. We mentally had imaged the Marines through this event a dozen times. They knew exactly what to expect and behaved as if they had been there before.

Fast forward six months. Here we were again on the very same tarmac. This time the Marines are combat veterans returning from Iraq with dozens of firefights behind them. Soon they would be reunited with family, friends, and significant others. It was a day they had dreamed of and had wondered many times if they would ever see it. The sergeant major and I were again with Kilo Company and remarked to each other that they looked the same. All were a little thinner, and their equipment was a bit more worn, yet it was still immaculate. They had every reason to act upbeat, even giddy. They had survived. Yet, they stood there stoically, waiting for the buses, equipment worn correctly, quietly talking to each other, faces expressionless. They had done this a dozen times—plus one.

SEVEN POUNDS OF PRESSURE

THE SOLDIER WHO CAN AND WILL SHOOT IS ESSENTIAL TO VICTORY IN BATTLE.

—BRUCE C. CLARK

I t takes seven pounds of pressure applied by the index finger to pull the trigger of an M-16A2 Service Rifle and initiate the cycle of functioning. In less than a heartbeat, the 62-grain M855 ball round with steel penetrator hurtles downrange at 3,100 feet per second and punches into another human being, ripping through soft tissue, bursting internal organs, and smashing bone.

The physical act of applying seven pounds of pressure is easy. But what does it take to put your front sight post on another human being and pull the trigger, knowing that in a split second you take from that person everything he has and has ever dreamed of doing?

The act of killing appears in masquerade in our society's media. In our celluloid version of killing, the mortally wounded "bad guy" clutches his chest and slumps to the ground with an appropriate spot of blood and perhaps a not-too-offending hole in his shirt. It is much different than that. To consciously think about your intended victim as a human being, to ponder the number of times that individual's mother must have fed and bathed him or her, to imagine that individual growing up, going to school, falling in love, and having a family—all shattered in an instant—can be debilitating. For this reason, killing is the ultimate taboo in Western society. Killing is not to be taken lightly. The cost of killing, the mental and emotional reckoning one must undergo afterward, can be incapacitating if not handled properly. How did we prepare our Marines to kill without hesitation, and then return to society with a clear conscience? This was another element of imaging we engaged in, and it is so important it warrants further discussion.

"I demand that you kill." I delivered those words to the battalion assembled in the base theater in 29 Palms, California, a month before we deployed. This was not a sophomoric attempt to rile the men, to whip them into some sort of frenzy. That would have been posturing and irresponsible. I spoke from the heart and solemnly.

In his seminal work *On Killing*, Dr. David Grossman detailed "The Anatomy of Killing." The anatomy of killing consists of several factors: training, conditioning, distance from the target, and the like. However, perhaps the most prominent factor for success in enabling men to kill is the leader's expectation for his men to kill. The leadership of the battalion discussed the rules of engagement with the men and ran countless shoot-don't-shoot drills, so that the Marines could recognize legitimate targets. In cases where we were unsure of a target, Marines would have to give the benefit of the doubt. This was a very fine line to walk—to kill without undue hesitation, yet not to kill what did not need killing. We *trained* the Marines to identify legitimate targets and *conditioned* them to kill them. It short, it was our desire to erase any hesitancy over whether or not to pull the trigger on a legitimate target. The battlefield is no place to debate the morality of killing. We did not wish to place too much "cotton" between the trigger and finger and breed timidity.

A corollary to the leader's demand to kill is to provide absolution for killing. We told the Marines that they were absolved of the deaths they would cause. When they killed legitimate targets within the rules of engagement, they would be praised. Their conscience should be clear and their honor clean as long as they acted within the rules of engagement and my intent and orders. We would not be killing as individuals, but as a cohesive unit. The burden of killing belongs to the commander. I was prepared to answer to my maker for the deaths that we inflicted. I believe it is incumbent upon the leader to relieve his men of the burden of guilt and self-doubt. A leader should have more emotional shock-absorbers than the 18-year-old private first class. Absorbing excess shock and guilt should be the role of the leader.

We did not try to dehumanize the enemy. I never heard derogatory terms used like "rag-head" or any other slurs. I certainly would not have condoned it. We simply called the enemy what they were: tanks, infantry, Fedayeen, or Muj, short for Mujahadeen. We did not need to create emotional distance from the fellow human beings we would be killing. Back in the 29 Palms theater, not on the battlefield, we had imaged our way through the act of killing; we already had made the decision to pull the trigger when we faced the enemy. We already had asked God to forgive us for what we were about to do to the Iraqi Army.

THE ROLE OF THE COMMANDER IN COMBAT

ONCE CONDITIONS BECOME DIFFICULT, AS THEY MUST WHEN MUCH IS AT STAKE, THINGS NO LONGER RUN LIKE A WELL-OILED MACHINE. THE MACHINE ITSELF BEGINS TO RESIST, AND THE COMMANDER NEEDS TREMENDOUS WILL-POWER TO OVERCOME THIS RESISTANCE. IT IS THE IMPACT OF THE EBBING OF MORAL AND PHYSICAL STRENGTH, OF THE HEART-RENDING SPECTACLE OF THE DEAD AND WOUNDED THAT THE COMMANDER HAS TO WITHSTAND FIRST IN HIMSELF AND THEN IN ALL THOSE WHO, DIRECTLY OR INDIRECTLY, HAVE ENTRUSTED HIM WITH THEIR THOUGHTS AND FEELINGS, HOPES AND FEARS. AS EACH MAN'S STRENGTH GIVES OUT, THE INERTIA COMES TO REST ON THE COMMANDER'S WILL ALONE.

—CARL VON CLAUSEWITZ, *ON WAR*

What makes a commander successful in combat? Why did Napoleon say, "There are no bad regiments—only bad Colonels"? Where does the commander belong on the battlefield? How does one steel oneself and develop the willpower to endure the ordeal that Clausewitz portrays in the above quotation? What are the elements of will? What are the attributes of a good leader in combat, and how does one develop those attributes in oneself? I do not pretend to have the definitive answers to these timeless questions, but I have spent years thinking about and studying them, and have put my own preparations to the test of combat. I submit them here for the reader's consideration.

Hearts and Minds

Thus, true strength of will in the commander develops from his study of human nature, for it is in the measure that he acquires knowledge of how other men think that he perfects himself in the control of their thoughts and acts.

—S.L.A. Marshall, *Men Against Fire*

My Division Commander, Major General James N. Mattis, told us "The most important battle a commander must win is for the hearts and minds of his men." He was 100 percent right. Once a commander has done that, once he has secured the affections of his men, the rest is simple. But how? Let's break it down, hearts and minds, one part emotion, one part logic. To win either, the commander must be an expert in understanding human nature.

Winning Hearts

However fine the weapon, however adequate the equipment; neither represents any more strength than the hearts of the men who use them.

—Matthew B. Ridgway

To win the hearts of your men you must win their affections. This is not accomplished by pandering to them or currying favor, but by treating them as men with respect, and also by being competent and fit. You must be another human to them, and they must know that their welfare is paramount to you, that their lives are as dear to you as your own. Finally, they must know that you exist to serve, not to be served. In short, you must love your men.

There exist a thousand barriers between a 40-plus-year-old lieutenant colonel and an eighteen-year-old private first class. Inside these barriers can lay mistrust, cynicism, and reservations. Only when these barriers are systematically broken down and common cause made between the commander and the individual Marine, can a unit function in true harmony—with mutual respect, amicable discipline, and an atmosphere of brotherhood.

In his book *Reminiscences of a Marine,* General John A. Lejeune captures the concept of smashing these barriers and winning hearts.

> To be a really successful leader, a senior officer must avoid aloofness. … He should not place himself on a pedestal and exercise command from a position far above the heads of his men, but he must come down to the ground where they are struggling and mingle with them as a friend and as a father. A word or two of sympathy and of praise spoken to… men exhausted from the stresses of combat may change depression to exaltation and, being spread about among the men may cause them to feel that their chief has their welfare at heart and he is full of human sympathy for them.[11]

As put by Major General T.S. Jones, USMC, this is "eyeball leadership." An effective commander must be able to move about the men and understand them, their thoughts, their hopes, and their desires. A simple hand on the shoulder, a touch on the elbow, a smile and a wink can speak volumes. However, Major General Jones always cautioned that these gestures must come with the following warning:

Warning: Without genuine concern all this is worthless.[12]

In the words of General Lejeune, "Men are quick to detect pretense or insincerity in their leaders, and worse than useless as a leader is the man in whom they find evidences of hypocrisy."[13] Once discovered, the hypocrite is finished as a leader. Men will not trust him, and he will not command their will or actions.

Winning Minds

> No matter what may be the ability of the officer, if he loses the confidence of his troops, disaster must sooner or later ensue.
>
> —Robert E. Lee

Winning hearts and minds through logic is the realm of work, of sweat and toil, of study and vigilance. The men must see their commander as competent in the art of war, so that they know he will not squander their lives with poor tactics, ill-advised policies, or hubris. The commander must "sell" his vision for the command to the men. True, there is no formal requirement for a commander to obtain a mandate from his men. The commander has every legal right to dictate the unit's actions. However, when the reality of war and its attendant hardships set in, and men become exhausted, deprived, and uncertain, the leader commands nothing if he does not first command their hearts and minds. Superficial relationships between leaders and their men that rely on the trappings of rank structure and protocol are as brittle as untempered steel that shatters on impact; its structure, seemingly stout when viewed from a distance, lacks the molecular structure that comes from tempering that lends it strength, flexibility, and hardness in the right measures.

The art of command is the practice of imposing one's will over the men of the unit, in a legal, ethical, and moral manner, without being a tyrant. It is to win their affections so fully that one can call upon them to willingly sacrifice themselves to accomplish the greater mission. Once a commander has won the hearts and minds of his men, he must strive to keep them every day, especially in combat.

How is this done? How does a commander impose his will on the men he commands? What does it take to succeed in the art of command in combat? Following is an attempt to answer these questions and to explain the rationale for how I attempted to prepare myself and the other leaders of the battalion. I will discuss preparing for command; the attributes I sought to develop in leaders; the concept of moral authority in combat; and developing, nurturing, and hardening one's own willpower.

Attributes of the Commander

> *[The leader's] most sacred duty is to purify his own soul, and to cast out from it all unworthy motives.*
>
> —John A. Lejeune

I sought to develop in the officers of the battalion, and in myself, the following attributes: force of personality, mentoring and coaching skills, social energy, and, finally, the virtue of shame. These attributes were at the center of winning the hearts and minds of the men and establishing a harmony of unity and brotherhood. These attributes were not a replacement for the time-tested "Leadership Traits and Leadership Principles" listed below. Rather, these attributes were a vehicle to put the traits and principles to work, a construct to help metabolize theory and intellectual understanding into action on a daily basis. We made them *habit*. They are the elemental building blocks of willpower.

Leadership Traits	Leadership Principles
• Judgment	• Know your people and look out for their welfare.
• Justice	• Keep your people informed.
• Decisiveness	• Know yourself and seek self-improvement.
• Initiative	• Be technically and tactically proficient.
• Dependability	• Seek responsibility and take responsibility for
• Tact	your actions.
• Integrity	• Make sound and timely decisions.
• Endurance	• Set the example.
• Bearing	• Develop a sense of responsibility in your
• Unselfishness	subordinates.
• Courage	• Ensure that the task is understood, supervised, and
• Knowledge	accomplished.
• Loyalty	• Train your people as a team.
• Enthusiasm	• Employ your unit in accordance with its capabilities.

Force of Personality

Warriors want leadership from strong, competent, forceful leaders, not from the weak and timid, regardless of their intellect. A leader possessing a force of personality gets things done. His presence creates a dynamic chain reaction that cuts through inertia and apathy. Without force of personality, the Fifth Habit of discipline is a mirage. When friction builds, and the situation teeters on the brink of chaos, the leader who has internalized a force of personality imposes his will on the situation and sets it right. This attribute embodies the traits of initiative, courage, bearing, decisiveness, and endurance. A leader possessing a force of personality displays a bias for action, makes decisions in a timely manner, seeks responsibility, accepts the consequences, and is highly competent at his job. At one time, "force" was evaluated in a Marine's fitness report, but no longer. That is a shame, because force of personality is the foundation of a commander's willpower, willpower that is vital if the commander is to sustain himself and his unit on the battlefield.

Force of personality is that element of leadership that is critical in difficult situations. I demanded that the battalion live up to some very high standards without compromise. I was not always very popular for it either. Insisting on the proper wearing of helmets and chinstraps at all times, rehearsing our battle drills over and over despite harsh conditions, and insisting on target feedback for all our live-fire weapons training were all vital in laying the foundation of discipline and building the Five Habits. Yet, force of personality has its limits. I had to choose very carefully the issues I would insist upon, and then in turn expend a considerable amount of energy in enforcing my will. Force of personality must be targeted on what the commander prioritizes as essential, never on pet peeves or whims.

Coaching and Mentoring Skills

The relationship between an officer and his men should be that of scholar and student.
—John A. Lejeune, *Marine Corps Manual*

Men need leaders, not tyrants. The <u>role of the officer</u> is to set the standards for the unit and individuals and then work to modify behavior within the unit to achieve the desired standard. I told the men of the battalion the very first time that I talked to them what my expectations of them were. I also told them what they could expect from me—that expectation was a two-way street. I vowed to give them my very best effort every day, and I expected the same from them. It was a contract. We would be tolerant of each other's mistakes. I told them that as long as they made mistakes of commission rather than omission, I would embrace that mistake. I would even embrace it twice! I explained that tough, smart, aggressive Marines will win and survive in combat, while timid, "Mother-may-I" types will hesitate and fail in combat. My regimental commander, Colonel Craig Tucker, said it best: "Do the right thing, at the right time, for the right reason, and you cannot go far wrong."

Solve a problem for your men, especially a personal problem, and you have won their hearts. S.L.A. Marshall commented: "It is never a waste of time for a commander to talk to his people about their problems; more times than not they will seem small to him, but so long as it looms large for the man it cannot be dismissed with the wave of a hand. He will grow in esteem of his men as he treats their affairs with respect." [14] This does not mean to molly-coddle the men with their problems. To the contrary, along with addressing the issue, you must coach and mentor them to solve their own problems.

Nobody was better at this than Sergeant Major Dave Howell. Admittedly, he was unvarnished and blunt. Among the many hard knocks that life had dealt him, he had been through three divorces, so you can imagine the "marriage counseling" he gave the young Marines. At the heart of his no-holds-barred counseling sessions was a genuine concern for his men, for he loved them—in a very rough way—and they loved him back. Many young men owe a debt of gratitude to Sergeant Major Howell for going well beyond the extra mile to take a genuine interest in their lives. He treated them as men and not as children, and demanded that they rise to the occasion. Under the attribute of coaching and mentoring skills, you will find judgment, justice, tact, and unselfishness as well as the leadership principle of knowing your people and looking out for their welfare. It is no more complicated than this. But, it is indispensable to breaking down barriers and making common cause with your people—and winning their hearts and minds.

Social Energy

> *Among the ever-pressing problems of the commander is the seeking of means to break down the natural [barriers] ... and give his men a chance to understand him as a human being rather than as an autocrat giving orders.*
>
> —S.L.A. Marshall, *Men Against Fire*

The exchange between Corporal Irish and me in the Al Kut palm grove after his wounding was a result of the social energy that flowed in the task force. There was an affinity for one another that transcended rank and responsibility. I have found that people will endure incredible hardship if two ingredients are in place. First, the leader endures the same hardship shoulder to shoulder with them. Second, the men know why the hardship is necessary. This is a simple enough concept, but it is so easy for a leader, beset by exhaustion and mounting tasks, to seek refuge in rank and position and dictate in the "because I said so" manner. The men will know when the situation is urgent and immediate obedience to orders is required. They will especially know urgency is needed and expected if their leader, who has established a track record of explaining the situation to them, is now barking go-and-do orders. The men are very forgiving in this respect.

Simply sharing a meal with the men, cleaning your weapon with them, taking part in physical exercise and labor, reduce the barriers between the men and their commander. Knowing that their commander has their welfare at heart, they will bear any burden and endure tremendous hardship willingly. They will seek only to make their leaders proud and acquit themselves honorably. This is the essence of cohesion.

The day before I relinquished command of 3rd Battalion, 4th Marines to my successor, I was walking through the quarterdeck of the command post building. The area was buzzing with activity. We had just returned to 29 Palms from our second tour to Iraq, and many of the members of the historic 3/4 Association were on hand for the change-of-command ceremony. I stopped to talk to a couple of the association's Vietnam-era veterans when Corporal Josh Lipe of Lima Company walked onto the quarterdeck. Corporal Lipe had just that day checked back into the unit from convalescence leave, healing from wounds received in action a month earlier. Despite wearing his protective goggles, Corporal Lipe had lost an eye to shrapnel from a roadside bomb. I had not seen him since his wounding, but had sent his mother, Barbara, a note letting her know how proud I was of Josh and how he had acquitted himself honorably the day he was wounded. I immediately broke off my conversation with the Vietnam vets and at once went to Lipe and hugged him. I asked him how he was doing and if he was all right. Corporal Lipe harbored not an ounce of self-pity. He was upbeat, just glad to be alive and back with his brothers again. As we talked, I had my hand on the side of Lipe's neck and looked him eye to eye. I asked him to tell me the story of his wounding and his trip home and not to spare the details. The encounter lasted several minutes, after which Corporal Lipe and I hugged once more, and he moved on about his business. When I turned to rejoin the veterans I had been speaking to, I was shocked, just as shocked as when Corporal Irish told me in the palm grove that he was sorry for getting hit. The veterans stood there with tears in their eyes. One came forward and embraced me. He told me his commander from Vietnam, Lieutenant Colonel Masterpool, loved them that way as well. He thanked me for caring for the Marines. A young man had just lost an eye, but his greatest comfort seemed to have been being back with his brothers again. Such social energy is priceless.

On the battlefield is where social energy resonates throughout a unit. During the battle for An Nasiriyah 23-26 March 2003, then-LtCol Royal Mortenson, Commanding Officer of 2nd Battalion 8th Marines, Task Force Tarawa, describes going to the wounded Marines in the middle of vicious firefight. "Several times I was able to move from my [command] vehicle and kneel down beside each wounded Marine. As I tried to reassure them I looked into their bloodied faces, our eyes met and they said only one thing, "I'm ok sir, let me go back to my squad." [15]

We found that social energy was an important salve in mitigating and treating post traumatic stress disorder (PTSD). The sense of family, and the mutual trust that ran horizontally and vertically through the unit were vital to providing an atmosphere in which we could deal openly with the emotions associated with PTSD. We explained to the Marines that if we were in a tight spot in a firefight, it was expected that one would call for supporting arms: tanks, artillery and close air support. No Marine ever fights alone. We extended this line of logic to the impact of PTSD: No Marine ever had to fight alone, and our "supporting arms" for this fight were found in brotherhood and concerned leadership.

Upon our return from our first tour in Iraq, a young Lance Corporal experienced acute symptoms of PTSD. We never sent him away from the unit, and he was fully integrated in everything we did. He remained in his squad and his squad mates accompanied him to counseling sessions. He recovered fully, a testament as much to his own strong character and resolve as anything else. He returned to Iraq with us for our second tour, this time as a fire team leader, and distinguished himself in battle at Fallujah and Al Karmah in 2004.

This attribute of social energy holds the traits of integrity, loyalty, and enthusiasm. Moreover, social energy communicates the virtue of humility in the leader—not the self-effacing humility of words, words that so often can ring hollow, but a humility communicated by deed.

The Virtue of Shame

> *The spirit of man springs from divinity. It is the God-like quality in man and through its workings in his heart, a transformation is wrought; buoyancy, courage, determination, forgetfulness of self, and love for comrades, his country and the organization to which he belongs dominates his whole being. In after life, he remembers that period of unselfishness and exaltation. It becomes the most sacred part of his life and he glories in the hardship and suffering he endured, the dangers he faced, the difficulties he overcame, the sacrifices he made, and the courage he displayed. In these memories, and in these only, lie "the glory of war."*
>
> —John A. Lejeune

Some may recoil from my use of shame as a commander's tool. However, it is a powerful catalyst, not in the sense of casting or projecting shame on a unit or individual in a shallow attempt to manipulate, but having a mature sense and understanding of human nature, emotions, and motivations. The above quote from General Lejeune is priceless. It captures what we all seek to become and frames the concept of shame as a positive catalyst, or virtue, that appeals to the higher attributes of humankind. Richard Ayers of the Center for Labor-Management Studies explains virtue as a "universal standard of right and wrong ... virtues unite us in community." [16] It is shame that prevents us from doing shameful things; it is shame that propels us forward despite fear, hunger, and sleeplessness. Shame is the knowledge that one's behavior or performance is less than what is expected by the group. Shame in the eyes of our brothers is a powerful motivator. No one wants to be known or remembered for coming up short when most needed.

"Afraid of fear—death holds no fear." [17]

Our greatest fear in battle was not death or maiming. It was the fear of being a coward in the eyes of our comrades. For leaders, the fear of showing weakness in front of one's men was more terrifying than any physical threat to life and limb. Everyone harbors doubts about their courage under fire, but the idea of being singled out as a coward is simply too much to bear. Shame is closely related to social energy and is another catalyst of cohesion. The earnest leader must understand this powerful human behavior and learn to tap its energy.

All men desire honor. They dream of one day being able to speak of the great deeds of their youth. None put forth this concept more eloquently than William Shakespeare in his timeless play *King Henry V*. The young king addresses the assembled mass of his hopelessly outnumbered army on the eve of the 1415 Battle of Agincourt:

If we are mark'd to die, we are enow to do our country loss; and if to live, the fewer men, the greater share of honor. ... That he which hath no stomach to this fight, let him depart. His passport shall be make, and crowns for convoy put into his purse. We would not die in that man's company that fears his fellowship to die with us. This day is call'd the feast of Crispian. He that outlives this day and comes safe home will stand a tip-toe when this day is named. ... Then will he strip his sleeve and show his scars, and say, "These wounds I had on Crispian's day." Old men forget ... but he'll remember with advantages what feats he did that day. ... We few, we happy few, we band of brothers. For he to-day that sheds his blood with me shall be my brother; be he ne'er so vile, this day shall gentle his condition; and gentlemen in England now a-bed shall think themselves accurs'd they were not here, and hold their manhoods cheap whilse any speaks that fought with us upon Saint Crispian's day.

(*King Henry V,* 4.5. 20–22; 35–67)

The commander must be able to tap into this desire from time to time to appeal to love for comrades and country. He must be able to conjure up the ghosts of our ancestors who sacrificed themselves for our way of life, our very freedom, and forecast the feelings of pride that will belong to the steadfast and sturdy of heart. He must cultivate and harness the lineage and pride of unit history. He must win hearts and minds. In the words of Scottish writer John Buchan, "The task of leadership is not to put greatness into humanity, but to elicit it, for the greatness is already there."

On 19 March 2003, at Camp Ripper, Kuwait, I stood on the ramp of an AAV with the task force gathered around me. This would be the last time I would be able to speak to them as a group before combat. In an hour we would be heading north to our dispersal area to await the final command to attack across the Kuwaiti border into Iraq. I did not give a rousing "Sands of Iwo Jima" speech, but I spoke firmly and soberly. I reminded them of their training, that we were not alone, and that the best way to come out alive on the other side was simply to do your duty to the best of our ability. I reminded them that we, as a Corps, exist for one reason—to win on the battlefield. The day the Marine Corps fails to win in combat is the day we will cease to exist. I reminded them that our ancestors from Tripoli, Belleau Wood, Guadalcanal, Iwo Jima, Inchon, Chosin, and Vietnam would be watching us. It was now our turn, our duty, to take our place in the line of history and fight well. I appealed to the pride of being a Marine. Up till now they had reaped all the benefits of wearing the uniform, the prestige and honor of belonging to such a storied fighting unit. I also wanted to give these young men, many less than a year out of high school, a sense of the history at hand. I told them that these next few days, weeks, and months would be the defining moment of their young lives, and their mates today would be their mates for the rest of their lives. How they conducted themselves would be the yardstick by which they would value themselves for a lifetime. "Give a good accounting of yourselves. Keep your honor clean. Acquit yourselves with honor. Do this and you will have peace the rest of your lives." The feeling of brotherhood was overwhelming. I knew I had won their hearts and minds, and they had won mine.

THE MORAL IMPERATIVE
OF COMMAND

OF EVERY ONE HUNDRED MEN IN BATTLE, TEN SHOULD NOT EVEN BE THERE. EIGHTY, ARE NOTHING BUT TARGETS. NINE ARE THE REAL FIGHTERS, WE ARE LUCKY TO HAVE THEM SINCE THEY MAKE THE BATTLE. AH, BUT THE ONE—ONE IS THE WARRIOR—AND HE BRINGS THE OTHERS HOME.

—HERACLES

Where are we? Are we among the 10, the 80, or the nine? Are we striving to be the one? What have we done by way of preparation, mental and physical, to qualify us for the one? Is it enough? If our preparation is limited to compulsory resident or nonresident enrollment in service schools and unit-directed training, then I submit we are failing to live up to the moral imperative of leading young Americans in battle.

The moral imperative of leadership is to prepare ourselves physically, morally, spiritually, and intellectually for the reason put forth by General John A. Lejeune: "Leaders must have a strong sense of the great responsibility of their office; the resources they expend in war are human lives." The sheer gravity of this responsibility is enough to warrant a monk-like existence of study in the art and science of war. Simply put, to meet our responsibilities as leaders requires serious study, beyond the basic career progression paths of our respective services. Nowhere is this truer than in the realm of human emotions and motivations and the cultivation of willpower.

I offer to the reader my own thoughts on preparation for command in war and the methods to put that preparation into practice in that laboratory of human emotion known as combat.

The 5,000-Year-Old Mind

Tactical errors [spell] not only failure, but unnecessary loss of human life . . . avoidable ignorance on the part of [leaders is] inexcusable and reprehensible . . . it [is] their bounden duty so to prepare themselves as to be able to lead their men in such manner as to achieve victory with minimum of loss.

—John A. Lejeune

I was a young captain when my Division Commander, then Major General P.K. van Riper, introduced the concept of a "5,000-year-old mind" to me. "With 5,000 years of recorded military history," he said, "there is no excuse for the lack of constant study." He was right. I had no excuse for my lack of study; I had been content to allow myself to rest on the education the Marine Corps provided for me. Of course, I had read military books and history, but I did not seriously study nor did I ask myself the hard questions of how to put such knowledge to work. My leadership training was passive. I was content with the traits and principles

taught to me as a second lieutenant and with the leadership lessons I had gleaned
from practical application. I was criminally content that I had done my part. I
did not study human nature and the hearts of men. I resolved that day to correct
my deficiency and have since read nearly everything I could get my hands on. I
pored over field manuals and training circulars. I studied philosophy, psychology,
and physiology. I read about the great captains and sought out mentors. I absorbed
everything I could from veterans, either from their writings or in conversation.
I admit to being a bit of an intellectual magpie. I even sought lessons on human
nature in poetry, plays, and sacred texts. In short, I cast my net widely. I had bought
into the moral imperative of command. I never wanted to look into the mirror and
face the fact that I had gotten men killed due to my self-imposed limitations as a
student of command. I cannot honestly say today that I do not harbor guilt over
my too-little-too-late self-education and the mistakes I made in combat, mistakes
retrieved only by the valor of my men.

The Dirty Little Secret of Combat

> *Education is the mother of leadership.*
> —Wendell Wilkie

The people we recruit are fantastic. Our young Soldiers, Sailors, Airmen, and
Marines, backed up by tremendous technology and firepower, always will get
the job done. The dirty little secret of combat is that these young Americans
will get the job done despite lackluster training and in spite of less-than-inspired
leadership. The difference between that group and a group that is well trained
and well led is the price of the butcher's bill in war. Lieutenant Colonel Howard
Christy, USMC (Retired), a Silver Star winner and veteran company commander
from Vietnam comments: "Indeed, human losses are often celebrated as much as
regretted. The more blood spilled, the more noteworthy the battle and, perhaps,
the more noteworthy the commander." [18] Christy is lamenting the commander
who serves himself and not his men, the commander who does not understand the
moral imperative of command and the intrinsic value of each individual human
life. Casualties will occur in combat, even when everything is done correctly and
the training is sound. But, as often as not, deaths and maiming are the result of
either the hubris of the leader who denies that he has tactical shortcomings, or a
deficit in the iron willpower required to control the actions of his men and enforce
discipline. My ideal of success was to win a fight without having to win a bunch of
medals in the process. If we could take objectives at "sling-arms" because we had
devastated the enemy with fires and maneuver, then great. In short, I never looked
for a fair fight.

The mere fact that a person is somehow a vetted "combat veteran" by virtue of service in a combat zone does not pass the logic test. A monkey that is shot at can speak with the same authority. Each is no more a warrior than an accidental victim. The experience of being shot at neither confers on the leader the distinction of all-knowing veteran nor relieves the leader of continuously learning, evaluating himself, and seeking self-improvement.

Colonel Craig Tucker, the Commanding Officer for Regimental Combat Team 7 for Operation Iraqi Freedom 2, saw self-study as the indispensable ingredient for a competent combat leader. "The ability to anticipate and the courage to take action on that belief is a critical task for the commander. Clausewitz called this *coup de'oeil* and counted it as a quality of genius, you either had it or you didn't." Tucker believes that through a combination of experience and dedicated study you can acquire this skill. "Essential to both study and experience is the desire to immerse yourself in study and … to reflect on what is read or what was experienced and then apply critical analysis." Tucker defines critical analysis as deductive study of cause and effect. "Over time, a disciplined commander develops an intuitive ability to rapidly analyze and forecast what will likely happen next and take actions to control that sequence of events" [19]

Colonel Tucker cuts right to the heart of the moral imperative of command. He lays the obligation to study squarely on the shoulders of leaders and those aspire to lead. Furthermore, he strongly advocates the imperative to go beyond just mere passive reading and develop the critical skills of, as Tucker puts it, "habits of thought and habits of action."

Like any unit, Task Force, 3rd Battalion, 4th Marines suffered shortcomings. Not all of us were fully committed to the profession of arms or our mission, and some leaders required extra incentive to lead and train to the standard prescribed. There were leaders who did not live up the moral imperative of leadership. We were not perfect tactically, and we made mistakes, myself included. I do not hold myself blameless in the shortcomings of the battalion. To the contrary, any lapse in performance or fortitude is owing to me personally or to my inability to impose my will on others. Still, the overwhelming majority of the battalion's Marines and Sailors were committed to the unit, each other, and the mission, and they cheerfully submitted themselves to harsh training. It was due to their indomitable spirit that we succeeded. This fact is never far from my thoughts.

THE COMMANDER ON
THE BATTLEFIELD

*IF YOU CAN FORCE YOUR HEART AND NERVE
AND SINEW TO SERVE YOUR TURN LONG AFTER
THEY ARE GONE, AND SO HOLD ON WHEN THERE
IS NOTHING IN YOU, EXCEPT THE WILL WHICH
SAYS TO THEM: "HOLD ON!"*

—RUDYARD KIPLING, *IF*

Commander's Internal Culminating Point

In his work *On War,* Clausewitz posits the concept of the "culminating point," the point where a unit should no longer advance since it can no further exploit an advantage. Beyond that point a unit may no longer be able to shoot, move, or communicate effectively. It is overextended and vulnerable. I submit to the reader that the same holds true for the commander. The mounting "debits" of the battlefield force him to keep withdrawing from his "well of fortitude" at a faster rate than he can replenish it. When his well is empty, when he is physically, mentally, spiritually, and intellectually spent, he has extended beyond his internal culminating point and is vulnerable to the ravages of fear, doubt, and timidity. When this happens, the unit grinds to a halt with him. Clausewitz comments: "Once that hold is lost [the commander's] courage can no longer revive the courage of his men, the mass will drag him down to the brutish world where danger is shirked and shame is unknown." [20]

The will of the commander is the heart that pumps blood to the sinews of the unit. I deliberately sought to understand where my own internal culminating point was and to harden myself physically and mentally to push it back. I began running marathons, then 50-mile ultra-marathons. I added mountaineering, since it was a dangerous, physically exhausting sport, and a sport where teamwork was vital. My partner and I twice made the summit of Mount Rainier. I added multi-day adventure races that involved continuous movement on foot, canoe, or mountain bike, and required precise navigating and decision-making while sleep deprived. I did all these things badly, very badly in some cases, but I learned something about my shortcomings and myself every time, and I pushed my culminating point back a bit further. I developed a mental endurance envelope that sheltered my "well of fortitude." It would later sustain me during the march to Baghdad.

Location of the Commander

There are two ways a leader ethically imposes his will on the Marines he leads into combat: through his moral authority as a leader and by setting expectations.

First, legal authority is granted by virtue of one's warrant or commission. But its capacity to inspire men on the battlefield is extremely limited. *Moral* authority is much more important, and it is established and cemented by leading from the front. Only by embracing the same hazards as the Marines and Sailors you lead, will you establish that critical bond of trust that is at the heart of a unit's fighting spirit. One must lead from within what General Ridgway called the "zone of aimed fire." Marines know that tough and potentially dangerous decisions are required in combat. Knowing that a decision was made from within the "zone of aimed fire" builds confidence that their leaders know what is actually happening first hand at the point of contact, and have committed them to a course of action with the best possible chance of success. Nothing breaks down the walls of doubt and hesitancy, and builds up the bonds of trust and affinity, faster than shared danger and hardship.

"I command, and you control." This was my guidance to Major Martin Wetterauer, the task force operations officer. Major Wetterauer was a tough, smart, aggressive officer fully competent in coordinating the actions of the task force in a fight. What is equally important is that we implicitly understood each other. The nexus of command and control is often difficult to pinpoint; the best place to command is frequently not the best place to control. We approached the problem in a couple of ways.

The first method was the division of labor between Major Wetterauer and me. I was very active in directing the scheme of maneuver, especially when time was of the essence—which was nearly always. But once the order was issued, I gave control to Wetterauer and moved forward to a place behind the lead platoon of the company executing the main effort. From there I had first-hand knowledge of the situation and could issue on-the-spot orders to the company commander, face to face, then relay instructions and real-time situation updates to Major Wetterauer, who could adjust the rest of the battalion to the flux of the battlefield.

A second method was the employment of "directed telescopes." This concept actively employed two of the most seasoned Marines in the battalion in the fight: the battalion gunner, CWO-2 Gene Coughlin, and Sergeant Major Howell, known as "Eyes One" and "Eyes Two," respectively. As "directed telescopes" or "friction busters," they rode with the other two companies or focused on locations or events that I knew would generate friction, such as the point where the battalion was conducting a passage of lines with another unit. Once I even embedded Gunner Coughlin in the flank company of an adjacent battalion to help deconflict fires and unit locations in a two-battalion coordinated attack. Eyes One and Two extended my view of the battlefield and reported directly to Major Wetterauer and myself. The rationale for this was that when a company gets into a fight, the first thing the company commander must do is deal with the fight. The "Eye" accompanying the company commander in contact could, in addition to maintaining overall situation awareness, provide rapid reporting to battalion. There was some good-natured bantering about the "Eyes" being imbedded "tattletales," but the company commanders, professionals as they were, employed the "Eyes" as assets rather than deterrents. We were blessed to have two cool-headed, tactically sound and savvy leaders to fill this role for the battalion.

During the battle for An Nasiriyah, 23-26 March 2003, then LtCol Royal Mortenson, Commanding Officer of 2nd Battalion, 8th Marines, Task Force Tarawa, was positioned forward in the zone of aimed fire while defending a vital bridge over the Euphrates River from repeated and vigorous enemy counterattacks. Colonel Mortenson describes his rationale for being forward. "The fight went on, I was able to observe Marines literally moving to the sound of the guns, wading into the enemy and killing him. I knew intuitively that this was the right spot to be; the bond and contract of leadership I had tried to instill in the battalion dictated that I share the danger." [21] Despite being pinned down by enemy fire for a few moments from time to time, and partaking in the fighting as a direct participant, from his position forward Colonel Mortenson gained unfiltered situational awareness at the point of decision and was able to coordinate and bring to bear not only the assets of the battalion but the air-ground task force to support the Marines as they closed the final yards on the enemy.

There is always some danger with the commander being too far forward and becoming a rifleman when pinned down. That happened to me at Al Kut, but all things considered, I would not change a thing. The trade-off for the handful of instances where I was pinned down was that I always had excellent situational awareness at the point of main effort and, as Colonel Mortenson demonstrated, was able to coordinate the application of combat power much more precisely. Furthermore, I believe that I gained moral authority by being with the men and fighting shoulder to shoulder. Nevertheless, even though the commander cannot hold his life and limbs as being any more precious than any other man in the unit, he must strike a balance and not needlessly endanger himself. Losing a leader in the midst of a fight can be debilitating. In the words of

S.L.A. Marshall, "A battalion, advancing boldly, may be brought in check because its commander did it the disservice of going too far forward and getting himself killed within sight of the ranks." [22] True enough, the easiest thing for a leader to do is get himself killed, and admittedly, I had some close calls. But we all did.

Second is the power of expectations communicated by vigorous enforcement of the basics and demonstrated in combat by personal example. In the battle of Thermopylae, the Spartan King Leonidas fought shoulder to shoulder with his band of 300 Spartans against the Persians and Xerxes' 10,000 Immortals. Leonidas chose to lead from within the phalanx, as a fellow hoplite in the second rank. With such an example, a unit will emulate a leader's will and aggressiveness to move on the enemy, and that aggressive spirit will permeate a unit. This is not to say that all leaders should be relegated to the role of a rifleman but, rather, to embrace the role of fighter/leader. This is particularly important for a unit in its first fight when men desperately need an example as a waypoint on which to measure their own actions.

I received criticism, not all of it constructive, for actively participating in firefights and throwing grenades. The criticism was centered on the thought that the role of the commander was to direct and coordinate the actions of the unit as a whole. That is true, and I am guilty as charged. My participation in the initial firefights, with the exception of Al Kut (since that was for survival) was intended to execute the attributes of a leader, as well as to command. By being forward, I was still coaching, still mentoring. Even though it was actual combat, we had never ceased to train.

Noted military historian John Keegan saw that the first and greatest imperative of command was the imperative of example. "Those who impose risk must be seen to share it." [23] Early on in the Iraq campaign it was vital to be forward in order to establish my expectations for aggressiveness in combat. The tremendous social energy gained in sharing danger cannot be overstated. It was a powerful incentive for Marines to give their best; it bred aggression and initiative. The officers, SNCOs, and NCOs all fought forward, and their aggressiveness propagated to the last PFC.

The practical reason for being forward is that the commander can make informed tactical and fire support decisions on the spot. General Ray Davis, winner of the Medal of Honor as a battalion commander at the Chosin Reservoir, remarked, "Oftentimes, a battalion commander can get fires quicker, especially if he is at the point of contact." I was able to compare my picture of the battle with that of my operations officer, Eyes One and Two, and my regimental commander.

There is another reason to have leaders forward. A key factor in Grossman's *Anatomy of Killing* involves the proximity of the leader to the individual that must do the killing. Grossman's studies found that the leader's close observation was critical in having men kill reliably. To that phenomenon, add the image of leaders, side by side with the Marines, actively killing as well, and you have the makings of a resolute and aggressive fighting unit.

"THE WARRIOR'S STONE MASK"

THE NAME OF THE GAME IS WAR. IF YOU GET
TOO CLOSE TO WAR, AND LOOK IT IN ITS EYES,
IT WILL TAKE YOU; MUSCLE, BRAIN AND BLOOD,
AND YOU WILL NEVER AGAIN KNOW JOY.
MARRIAGE, CAREER AND FAMILY WILL ALL BE
DISAPPOINTMENTS.

—KENT ANDERSON, SYMPATHY FOR THE DEVIL

The commander in combat is often an enigma to his men, a Sphinx-like being, seemingly placid amid the carnage of combat, immune to the heartrending scenes of destruction, the screams of the wounded, and cries of civilians who have just lost every possession and often the lives of their loved ones. The commander appears to have a split personality—one moment being indifferent to the point of heartlessness and the next moment being caring and self-sacrificing. He seems able to blend impossible expectations with heavy dollops of cruelty, seemingly without conscience or memory.

The leaders we admire in our history seem to possess this stoic, Sphinx-like quality. The paragons of this are General George Washington crossing the Delaware, confident and poised; General Robert E. Lee at Gettysburg sending Pickett's division to near annihilation at the Angle; General George Patton driving the 3rd Army through a winter storm in the Ardennes to relieve the beleaguered garrison at Bastogne; or Colonel Lewis B. Puller driving his regiment through the mountains surrounding the Chosin Reservoir in sub-zero weather to defeat several Chinese divisions. I submit that these noble images are partly a façade, a very necessary and carefully nurtured façade—the Stone Mask required to function under the pressures of command in war. Clausewitz poignantly described the weight these men bore: "The deep anxiety which he, [the commander] must experience works on his strength of will and puts it to the test ... for he is answerable to himself alone." [24]

In ancient cultures, warriors wore actual masks in battle to project a menacing appearance to the enemy and to inspire comrades. Worn over the face, masks not only hide your true identity and emotions from the outside world, but project an entirely different being, camouflaging any fear in the warrior's heart or doubt in his eyes. The mask also protects the wearer: The commander will not be betrayed by sympathy or compassion, and, seemingly, will remain untouched by the devastation and human suffering around him.

In the sustained combat during the march to Baghdad, I discovered the mask. I found comfort in the mask; it was a valuable tool that allowed me to remain focused on the task at hand. But once the fighting had stopped, I didn't take off the mask. I liked the mask: It was safe, and, in a subconscious way, I sought refuge in it. The Mask granted me immunity from my conscience; to take it off would have been to submit to the backlog of emotion and analysis. I tried to take it off, several times, like a bandage, one hair at a time. For me the bandage finally was torn off all at once. I was home with my wife, enjoying leave after the battalion had redeployed home. I was reading the Op-Ed pages in the *Washington Post* and ran across an editorial authored by a fellow battalion commander, Lieutenant Colonel Jim Seaton. This article was powerful for two reasons. First, it graphically represents the conflicted emotions of combat and the conflicting duties of the battlefield commander. On the one hand, you have a duty as a commander to see to your mission and men. On the other hand, you have a duty as a human being to aid the helpless. Seldom will Mars allow you to tend to both. Second, the piece illustrates the exogenous, or "debit," factors of the battlefield that assault the senses and the conscious, gradually wearing away one's will—unless the commander wears a mask. Seaton describes his artillery battalion's drive to Al Kut north on Highway 7 where he comes across a small boy mortally wounded on the road.

> It was a boy of 5 or 6. His eyes were closed and he was dead or dying. I bent over, gently cupping his left cheek and chin with my right hand. He was alive, and my touch must have startled him; both arms fluttered before settling again by his sides. ... I yelled at Marines in passing vehicles, asking if they had a corpsman present, but they continued. ... It was only a minute or so, but it felt much longer. Nobody stopped, and I knew why. We were on the attack. ... And my heart ached at what I was about to do. Thinking of my own children, I slowly stood up, leaving my hand on his face until my arm was completely extended. I left that gravely wounded boy, alone, lying there in the middle of the road as monstrous armored vehicles roared by. [25]

"The Boy by the Side of the Road" was the tipping point where, all at once, I fully understood and surrendered the mask. The article is potent and shows how the nature of combat is at once voracious and capricious, a domain where compassion is seldom rewarded. Indeed, it is often punished, not by any penal system, but rather by bleeding emotional energy from you when you have none to give. Compassion is frequently punished by making your men vulnerable to ruses by the enemy, such as false surrender or posing as civilians that exploit the chivalry of your men and seek to lure them to their deaths. That can be the high price of compassion.

Let us confront one issue head-on and spare each other blushes on the subject of killing. I participated in killing both directly, by taking life myself, and indirectly, through orders to the battalion. I never felt pity or compassion in killing the enemy. Instead, I was intoxicated by the thrill of the fight, as war removed its own Mask of glory and romance and revealed to me its true face of fleshless bone, and the dark side of man—and perhaps myself. I have always known that the dark side was there, always just out of sight, like the figure you see from the corner of your eye, but is gone when you turn to face it. Except this time, when I turned, it *was* there, and it was a vicious face. As for killing the enemy, I never had and never will have remorse for that. In fact, I drew gratification from it then and still do. But that doesn't stem from blood lust; it is more akin to the satisfaction a sheep dog must feel after having successfully defended the flock from a predator. An embedded reporter asked me after a firefight in Afak, during which I killed two enemy fighters attempting to fire into our flank, how I felt about it. My response was no more profound than an expression of having been "proficient" at an everyday task, a business transaction. Now, nearly two years removed from that day, my feelings have not changed.

Like Jim Seaton, I too saw children maimed and killed. I, however, did not feel anything, nor was I moved to act. I abandoned what may have been my duty as a fellow human being and continued forward into the attack, doing my duty as a commander. Later, I was shocked at my own indifference, at the ease with which I looked at the most pitiful sight imaginable and shrugged it off. Later, as the edges of my Mask began to peel back, I doubted my own humanity. After all, how could I not feel for my *own* experience with a boy by the side of the road? He was missing his jaw and nose and desperately clinging to life as it ebbed in a bloody froth. His mother pleaded for help in a language I did not need in order to grasp her agony. There was a slow, sinking realization that I might be one of the 2 percent of the population who is remorseless in killing. I felt a deepening disappointment that I was not the person I had hoped I was. I had hoped I was someone who cares for his fellow man and wants to make a difference. This is why I joined the Marine Corps. Instead, I was afraid that I was no different from Saddam's henchmen we had been killing, that I was just in a different uniform.

That summer Sunday morning, at my kitchen table, reading the paper, the mask came off all at once. Reading "The Boy by the Side of the Road" I was moved to tears, partly because of the tragic nature of the story and partly because I too am a parent and can at least in small measure imagine the pain and angst the mother must have felt. But, most of all, I wept because I did feel something after all, and I shed tears of relief, relief that I do have my humanity and that I am what I thought I was. My indifference to suffering had been nothing more than a stone mask, an emotional flak jacket to prevent such pitiful scenes from robbing my body and mind of the precious energy and conviction I needed to keep my own men alive.

Unknowingly, we burden our young warriors with the images of Washington, Lee, Patton, and Puller, the unattainable examples of soldierly virtue. Deep down, every prospective commander wonders if he can measure up and harbors more than a bit of doubt that he can. We fail to tell our young warriors about the mask, and how they must begin to construct their own masks from the very first day in uniform. They must study war and its affects on men, and they must make their bodies and minds resistant to fatigue and stress. If they do this, and one day they find themselves at the confluence of fate, circumstance and history with lives in the balance, they will not fail.

CONCLUSION

THE ART OF COMMAND

*ART (ÄRT), [ART, ARTE; ARTE; ARTICULATE] 1.
HIGH QUALITY OF CONCEPTION OR EXECUTION,
AS FOUND IN WORKS OF BEAUTY; AESTHETIC
VALUE. 2. A TRADE OR CRAFT THAT APPLIES
SUCH A SYSTEM OF PRINCIPLES AND METHODS
3. SKILL THAT IS ATTAINED BY STUDY, PRACTICE,
OR OBSERVATION. SKILL ARISING FROM THE
EXERCISE OF INTUITIVE FACULTIES.*

WEBSTER'S NEW WORLD DICTIONARY

A rt is defined as a superior skill that may be learned by study, practice, and observation. An aspiring student of the fine arts seeking to master the discipline will study its mediums of clay, stone, paint and canvas. He will practice and become expert in the use of brush and chisel. He may observe and emulate the great masters, imitating the mechanics of specific brush strokes or the subtle nuances of light and shadow. Yet he may never achieve art, not until he is able to express his intuition will it be called art. The same is true for the art of command in combat.

The third definition of art stated above, "Skill that is attained by study, practice, or observation. Skill arising from the exercise of intuitive faculties," is the crux of the art of command in combat. Throughout this work I have discussed the art of command. It is on the battlefield that the commander wields the tools and expresses his will and intuition through example and by establishing his moral authority to lead his men to achieve his envisioned endstate. Only after dedicated study, practice, and reflection is the commander ready to apply his art, his will and intuition to the canvas of battle. But Mars demands tribute in blood and treasure, and it is here where our art becomes the *dark* art of command, *dark* art that requires a special quality of toughness not required in any other vocation.

I have borrowed the concept of mental toughness from the great football legend Vince Lombardi. For Lombardi, the definition of mental toughness was not only the ability to take pain, but also the ability to inflict it. Combat leaders, you must be mentally prepared to inflict pain not only on the enemy, but also to indirectly inflict suffering on their men, who must go in harm's way.

The Passion of Command

> *The bravest are surely those who have the clearer vision of what is before them, glory and danger alike, and yet notwithstanding, go out to meet it.*
>
> —Thucydides

General Robert E. Lee stated that an effective commander must love his men, but he must also be prepared to order the destruction of the very thing he loves. That is not just prose. This paradox captures the essence of combat leadership. It is the heart of the art of command. On a conscious level, most commanders comprehend that burden, but the question remains: Are we mentally and emotionally prepared for such demands? Before the first shot is fired, the leader must look squarely in the mirror and gather the moral strength necessary to order his men into harm's way, to see them killed and maimed, to look into the eyes of the wounded and upon the faces of the dead, yet not lose his fighting spirit. Moreover, the true test is to look oneself in the mirror *after* young men who trusted their commander are killed and maimed, and do it all over again without losing the will to violently close with the enemy. Such force of will requires supreme mental toughness and strong "emotional shock absorbers" to rebound from these devastating blows while maintaining one's convictions. It requires enormous grit to weather such anguish and not detach oneself from the deep feelings of affinity and love for one's men. The commander who severs that link forfeits the vital buttress of brotherhood formed in shared danger and sacrifice that binds him to his men and makes war bearable. He will soon find himself alone, increasingly drawing from his "well of fortitude" until the bucket comes up dry, and his will shatters. Once this happens, the commander ceases to inspire and lead; his unit becomes a formless mass of souls bereft of the sense of shame that enables men to bear war's horror yet persevere with honor. He becomes a mere spectator to the slaughter of his men.

In short, the art of command is about winning the love of one's men, and then some day having to use that love to have them willingly risk terrible injury or death and violently take the lives of others. The skill and respect necessary to apply this art must be nurtured in peacetime through study of the human psyche both in combat and through vicarious experience. The passion to command is embodied in the commander's willpower, his love for his men, and personal aggressiveness in battle.

The love for his men is what allows a commander to apply and maintain his will power, and the conviction and aggressiveness to close with the enemy. He must be able to literally and figuratively look himself in the mirror each day of combat and know he had earnestly applied himself and had nurtured a passion for command. With a melancholy rigor he must apply himself in the serious study of warfare, its affects on those who fight, and earn the moral authority that grows from leading in the "zone of aimed fire." I will always harbor doubts over my efforts prior to and during combat, whether or not my personal preparation and leadership was all it could be. For the rest of my life—each time I look in the mirror I will be acutely reminded of my shortcomings, and a piece of my heart will chip away, for in the shadows of my eyes I will see their faces, staring back at me—for the rest of my life.

Anderson, Kent. *Sympathy for the Devil.* Garden City: Doubleday, 1987.

Clausewitz, Carl von. *On War.* Princeton, NJ: Princeton University Press. 1984.

Grinker, Roy R., and John P. Spiegel. *Men Under Stress.* New York: [PUBLISHER], 1963.

Holmes, Richard. *Acts of War: The Behavior of Men in Battle.* New York: Simon and Schuster, 1985.

Kaplan, Robert D. *Warrior Politics: Why Leadership Demands a Pagan Ethos.* New York: Vantage Books, 2002.

Keegan, John. *The Mask of Command.* New York, New York: Viking Penguin Inc., 1987.

Lejeune, John A. *Reminiscences of a Marine.* 1930. Reprint, Quantico, VA: Marine Corps Association, 1990.

Marshall, Samuel L. A. *Men Against Fire: The Problem of Battle Command in Future War.* 1947. Reprint, Gloucester, MA: Peter Smith, 1978.

McNab, Chris. *The SAS Mental Endurance Handbook.* Guilford, CT: Lyons Press, 2002.

Ridgway, Matthew B. *Soldier: The Memoirs of Matthew B. Ridgway* New York: Harper & Brothers, 1956.

[1] Operant training encourages learning to exert a positive influence over our environment. It is key in avoiding aversive conditioning and the learned helplessness and fear that go with it.

[2] Robert D. Kaplan, *Warrior Politics: Why Leadership Demands a Pagan Ethos* (New York: Vintage Books, 2002), p. 118.

[3] Roy R. Grinker and John P. Spiegel, *Men Under Stress* (New York: [PUBLISHER], 1963) p. 44, quoted in Richard Holmes, *Act of War: The Behavior of Men in Battle* (New York: Simon and Schuster, 1985), p. 137.

[4] David Grossman, *On Killing: The Psychological Cost of Learning to Kill in War and Society* (New York: Little, Brown, Back Bay Books, 1995), p. 84.

[5] David Grossman, Lecture delivered at USMC Amphibious Warfare School, Quantico, VA, 18 August 2000.

[6] Phillip Skuta, letter to author, 15 June 2005.

[7] Carl von Clausewitz, *On War,* ed. and trans. Michael Howard and Peter Paret (Princeton: Princeton University Press, 1984), p. 122.

[8] Harry D. Tunnell IV, letter to author, 12 June 2005.

[9] Tunnell

[10] Tunnell.

[11] John A. Lejeune, *Reminiscences of a Marine* (1930; reprint, Quantico, VA: Marine Corps Association, 1990), pp. 307–8.

[12] T. S. Jones, Speech delivered at USMC Amphibious Warfare School, Quantico, VA, 2000.

[13] Lejeune, *Reminiscences,* p. 307.

[14] Samuel L. A. Marshall, *Men Against Fire: The Problem of Battle Command in Future War* (1947; reprint, Gloucester, MA: Peter Smith, 1978), pp. 171–72.

[15] Royal Mortenson, letter to author, 6 June 2005.

[16] Richard Ayers, interview with author 22 July 2005

[17] Holmes, *Acts of War,* p. 206.

[18] Christy, "Imperatives of Real Military Leadership," *Marine Corps Gazette,* 88, no. 11 (2005), p. 82. I owe a great deal of gratitude to Al Christy. His "Imperatives" piece and many long discussions provided much of the intellectual grist and rigor to this monograph, and his use of the writings of both General John A. Lejeune and General Matthew Ridgway added depth, scope and focus to my work.

[19] Craig Tucker, e-mail to author, 23 June 2005.

[20] Clausewitz, *On War,* p. 105.

[21] Mortenson.

[22] Marshall, *Men Against Fire,* p. 179.

[23] John Keegan, *The Mask of Command* (New York, New York, Viking Penguin Inc. 1987) p.329.

[24] Clausewitz, *On War,* p. 104.

[25] James B. Seaton III, "The Boy by the Side of the Road," *Washington Post,* 31 August 2003, p. B07.

Other books published by the Marine Corps Association

The U.S. Marines and Amphibious War
By Jeter A. Isely and Philip A. Crowl

The Reminiscences of a Marine
By MajGen John A. Lejeune

The Soldier's Load and Mobility
of a Nation
Col S. L. A. Marshall

Fighting General
Biography of Gen Holland M. Smith
By Norman V. Cooper

Old Gimlet Eye
By Lowell Thomas

Infantry in Battle
The Infantry Journal, Inc.
Col George C. Marshall

Battle Leadership
By Capt Adolf Von Schell

Unaccustomed To Fear
By Col Roger Willock

Rifleman Dodd
By C.S. Forester

From The Horse's Mouth
Selected Thoughts On Small-Unit
Leadership
By Major Ted McKeldin

Guidebook For Marines

The Armed Forces Officer
Col S. L. A. Marshall

On Going To War
A Marine Lieutenant's Korean
War Experience
By LtGen Bernard E. Trainor

A Hero Among Heroes
Jimmie Dyess and the 4th Marine Division
By Perry M. Smith

Patriot Dreams
The Murder of Colonel Rich Higgins
By LtCol Robin Higgins

Leatherneck Square
Poems by Richard C. Schulze

Leatherhead in Korea
By SSgt Norval E. Packwood, Jr.

Mastering Tactics
A Tactical Decision Games Workbook
By Maj John F. Schmitt

Parade Rest
Protocol and Social Customs for Marine
Officers and Spouses

Roses and Thorns
A Handbook for Marine Corps
Enlisted Wives

To order or for more information on the Marine Corps Association Bookstore, please call, toll-free 1-888-237-7683 or visit us online at www.mca-marines.org